Praise for *Don't Blow the Interview*

"Here's how to prepare—and carry out—the winning interview for your successful job search, whether you're a recent graduate or a veteran of the job market. This concise, on-target book tells you all you need to know to land the position you really want."
—Marshall Loeb, CBS Radio commentator, senior columnist at MarketWatch, and former managing editor at *Fortune* and *Money* magazines

"Applicants who read this book and follow Mr. Ferrone's advice are the quality individuals that organizations like L-3 Communications hire. This book has the real *secrets* to being hired—all the *secrets* to getting the job that the other books left out. If you want to be a winner, this is the book you want!"
—Frank C. Lanza, chairman and CEO of L-3 Communications

"Who ever said that a career-strategy book has to be dull! Ralph Ferrone has blown a breath of fresh air into the most important room you may ever sit in—the interviewer's office. No one will ever need to be unprepared for that crucial interview with this wise, pithy, and indispensable guide at your elbow. Read this and the next words you may hear are, 'You're hired!'"
—Landon Jones, former managing editor of *People* and *Money* magazines

"I have interviewed hundreds of candidates in my thirty-plus years in the advertising business. I wish all the prospects had read this book! Job candidates, young or experienced, will find this book essential reading. It's all here, from developing an effective résumé through post-interview follow-up. Interviewers too should read *Don't Blow the Interview*. The interview questions alone are invaluable."
—Carl Kotheimer, partner of H̲o̲r̲i̲

"The author distills the essence of prepara
ple, common-sense, easy-to-follow strate

a must-read, especially for all graduating students. Those seeking employment should invest the time to learn how to market themselves to prospective employers. This book is one of the best investments you can make in your future."

—Mark Klein, CEO of Ladenburg Thalmann

Don't Blow
the
Interview

Don't Blow the Interview

How to Prepare, What to Expect, and How to React

Ralph Ferrone

 St. Martin's Griffin ⚇ New York

DEDICATION

This book is in memory of my very special son, Casey.

I always admired your strength and character.

To my wonderful and caring daughter, Katie,

whom I treasure and adore.

To my best friend and loving wife, Cathy.

You are the sunshine of my life.

To my brother Dennis, thanks for being a pal;

and to his family, Anne and Skyler.

I love you all very much.

————————

www.stmartins.com

Photo © Carl Kotheimer

Book design by Maura Fadden Rosenthal / Mspace

Library of Congress Cataloging-in-Publication Data

Ferrone, Ralph.
   Don't blow the interview: how to prepare, what to expect, and how to react / Ralph Ferrone.
      p.   cm.
   ISBN 0-312-34340-X
   EAN 978-0-312-34340-8
   1. Employment interviewing.   I. Title.

   HF5549.5.I6F47 2006
   650.14'4—dc22   2005052097

First Edition: February 2006

10   9   8   7   6   5   4   3   2   1

Interviewing can be a humbling experience. . . .

Often the test is taken before the lesson is learned.

Interviewing knowledge and skills are

the gateway to the job market.

They will contribute to your success or failure and

your ability to proceed beyond the initial interview.

So, *don't blow the interview!*

Contents

Preface

Many people in business widely acknowledge that individuals often do themselves a disservice during a job search because of inadequate interviewing skills.

In a concise and clearly presented format, *Don't Blow the Interview* prepares people for the interview process through an understanding of *what to expect* and *how to react*. This information is designed to be easily digested and quickly implemented.

While college students and early job seekers are in most need of direction in sorting out the interview process, the contents of this book can be helpful to any level job seeker.

Don't Blow the Interview has been presented to colleges and universities and represents "one-stop shopping": All the elements that are necessary for the entire job search process are incorporated in this one book.

The objective is to provide a solid foundation for approaching an interview with confidence. Everything is intended to give you that competitive edge. The following are the key elements of the objective.

To provide:
—A comfort level for the interview experience
—Familiarity with pre-interview, interview, and post-interview procedures
—Awareness of:
    –How to prepare
    –What to expect
    –How to react
    –Techniques
    –Etiquette

How This Book Is Structured

Whether you are already a member of the business world, a recent college graduate, or someone who's about to graduate, *Don't Blow the In-*

terview is intended to help you with that next step—securing a new job or getting your first one.

For simplicity's sake, the words "business" or "company" are used generically to include all fields: education, medicine, nonprofit, social services, law, creative arts, etc., as well as traditional business.

Regardless of which career path you choose, the interview process will have a similar purpose and that is to identify the most qualified candidates for a given job. Your goal is to be part of that short list—and ultimately the person selected.

To most effectively present this information, the contents of this book have been divided into five parts. The Introduction and Part 1 "tell the story" of how to go about obtaining and acing an interview, while Parts 2 through 5 contain all the sample materials you'll need to help you prepare on your own throughout the process.

Note: While some companies actually exist, others have been created by the author for illustration purposes only. In all cases personal names, addresses, phone numbers, etc., are fictional. Any similarities are purely coincidental and unintentional.

Don't Blow
the
Interview

Introduction:
Interviewing Logic and Rationale

Understanding the Interview Process

It is important to understand that looking for a job is a very competitive task, and should be treated as such. It is a game where the "players"—the job seekers—compete and the winner takes all.

For that reason you will see the phrases "competitive edge" and "competitive advantage" mentioned throughout this book. It is a quality that can provide a significant advantage over competing applicants who perhaps do not have this information, and do not realize that an interview is more than just a conversation, but rather a meeting with a very specific direction and purpose. Individuals possessing the proper interview knowledge will immediately stand out as more polished and savvy, and will increase their success potential.

To begin, you may not have thought of a job search in terms of marketing, advertising, and sales, but they are key to bringing a product to market. In this case, the product is you!

To that end, it is important to let potential buyers (employers) know that you are "for sale," and what your value is to them. To do so, you should put in motion a plan to present yourself accordingly.

Just as an attractively packaged product on a store shelf is more likely to catch your eye compared to ones that are bland or similar to one another, your goal should be to stand out from the crowd.

Therefore, you must devise a plan to effectively package and market yourself. Take your lead from marketing professionals and use these key points to help organize your thoughts and form a strategy:

1. **Establish Awareness:** Spread the word. Let employers know that you are "for sale" by distributing your cover letter and résumé to a target list of employers that are of most interest to you.

2. **Create Curiosity:** Since your cover letter and résumé (perhaps portfolio and/or CD, as well) are your advertising messages, and your only sales tools at this time, be sure that your accomplishments and experiences are clearly showcased to enhance the potential of catching the employer's attention and interest. This is the beginning of the packaging and marketing process that will enable you to stand out from the crowd.

   Employers are looking for indications of leadership qualities and individuals who were not merely satisfied with performing minimally in previous jobs or exams.

Accomplishments	Experiences
Dean's List	Previous business positions
Honor Society	Intern/externships
High grade point average (3.0+)	Volunteer work
Student government	Etc.
College organizations	
Varsity sports	

3. **Stimulate Involvement:** Hopefully the employer is now sufficiently curious to see if you are as impressive in person as you appear on paper. If so, the interview process is about to begin. As curiosity leads to involvement, it is time for the buyer (employer) to examine the "product" first hand. This is your opportunity to build on the positive impression that you made with your cover letter and résumé, and sell yourself. The face-to-face interview now becomes your best sales tool and allows you to put it all together.

   The key points to sell are:

   > Physical appearance
   > Body language
   > Verbal skills
   > Confidence level
   > Logic and reasoning
   > Personality

4. **Action:** This is where the buyer (employer) takes action—you are either passed on for another interview, hired, or rejected. If you are hired or passed on, you have succeeded. Certainly no one

likes to be rejected, but it happens. It is part of life. Sometimes it may be for reasons beyond your control. Perhaps your qualifications did not fully match the job requirements. In other cases there may be interviewing inadequacies that are within your control to correct. And that is the essence of this book.

By knowing *what to expect* and *how to react* you will increase your interviewing potential considerably. So, let's begin.

Maximize Your Expense and Effort

Don't Blow the Interview is intended to help you maximize the energy, expense, and effort you've already invested in yourself (through paying for and attending college, and/or in your prior and current employment) by providing a comfort level for the interview experience through an awareness of *what to expect* and *how to react*; the procedures, preparation, techniques, and etiquette that are key to a successful interview.

If you would like to capitalize on your earlier efforts and establish a competitive edge, this book will help you prepare for the interview experience. Remember, all you need to know is *what to expect* and *how to react*. It is the cornerstone of the foundation.

First, it is useful to compare the competitiveness and selectivity that exists in the job market to the college admissions process—an experience that most of us are familiar with.

For example, a college may receive five thousand applications and offer enrollment to twenty-five hundred students. For a variety of reasons the other twenty-five hundred do not qualify and are rejected. (Since not all invitations are accepted, about six hundred will eventually comprise the freshman class.)

The same process applies to the job market, where a high number of résumés may be received for only a few openings. For you to be considered for an interview, your résumé must be impressive, and your cover letter concise, well composed, and intriguing. These elements are important to catch the attention of the human resources (HR) person (or department head) who reviews a high volume of such correspondence daily.

Note that while human resource people are looking for the best applicants, the weeding-out process begins with negatives, ranging from an unimpressive background to a poorly composed cover letter, a cluttered résumé, or spelling or grammatical errors. Any of these are enough to have your correspondence end up in the circular file—a kind expression for the trash basket.

Second, be aware that a word, an action, the wrong question, or no question can all be reasons for an unsuccessful interview. Undetected, these mistakes can be repeated, while job opportunities slip by.

Assuming you have been successful in securing an interview, it is critical to be completely familiar with the process—otherwise any number of things can trip you up and blow the interview—and just as abruptly end your relationship with that particular employer.

I remember attending a luncheon in the Grand Ballroom of New York's Waldorf Astoria Hotel, where students from around the country were being honored for academic excellence. One of the speakers quickly caught the attention of the audience when he stated that upon graduating college, he went on sixty interviews before receiving his first job offer. Sixty interviews! He proceeded to explain that this was strictly a function of not understanding what to do and say, and that he would have succeeded much earlier had he possessed this information.

It is within your power to avoid such mistakes through awareness and knowledge.

Third, often a fear of the unknown can be very intimidating and un-settling. However, once a familiarity and a comfort level are established, whatever was causing this fear and anxiety can actually be transformed into an opportunity. A competitive advantage.

This is certainly true of interviewing, where, if armed with the proper knowledge, you can stand out from the crowd of individuals who do not know how to effectively navigate the process and respond.

So, let's put this information to work, create your competitive advantage, and increase your success potential.

The Competitive Edge

The benefits of understanding the interview process are very straight-forward:

—The greater your knowledge, the more confident you will be.

—The more confident you are, the greater your interview success.

—The greater your interview success, the greater your potential for faster job placement.

It is a classic chain reaction process. Confidence, confidence, confidence; once achieved new heights can be reached. We see it in sports all the time. Like sports, interviewing is a competition.

Part 1

Six Steps to Interview Success

Now that a rationale for a solid understanding of the interview process has been laid out, it is time to give you step-by-step information that will help prepare you for the interview.

There are six steps to interviewing success that will provide a concise and significant competitive edge.

1. Preparing a résumé
2. Obtaining an interview
3. What to do after scheduling the interview
4. Preparing for the interview
5. The interview
6. Post-interview follow-up

Step 1
Preparing a Résumé

What to Include

Your résumé will be the initial impression you make. It should be a complete description of your experiences and accomplishments, whereby providing an employer with a picture of who you are and what you have done. When preparing one, there are three formats from which to choose:

- —**Chronological** is the style and format that is most often used by students who are graduating and seeking their first jobs or internships, or those in the work force with limited experience.

- —**Functional** is intended to focus on more extensive and broader experiences and/or to mask gaps in employment; it is also appropriate for individuals changing careers.

- —**Chronological/Functional** is a combination of the two. This is a good choice to emphasize qualifications.

Multiple examples of all these formats can be found in Part 2 of this book (page 51).

Where possible customize the objective to include a benefit to the employer. For example: "To secure a head teaching position in elementary education for the purpose of providing students with a stimulating and enjoyable learning experience." As opposed to the stereotypical "To secure a teaching position at the elementary level."

This is an actual example that allowed the employer to appreciate the candidate's enthusiasm and interest for seeking this position for the right reasons, and allowed the individual to separate themselves from the bulk of prospects with generically stated objectives. Clearly both the employer and the candidate benefitted.

Home (and/or college) addresses and phone numbers should be listed at the top of the résumé along with your name and be labeled "permanent" and "temporary" where appropriate; and of course your cell phone number (if you have a cellular phone) and e-mail address should also be included. Make it easy for potential employers to contact you. (For example, see page 57.)

Be sure that your e-mail address projects the right image and is suitable for business. Do not use one that is adolescent or silly, such as hot-dog, mrcool, tampababe, etc. Also check your outgoing cell phone message: It should be concise and professional.

If you were involved in activities during or after college, list them; it shows that you have expanded your interests, and perhaps developed a better appreciation for teamwork—an important subject that will be discussed at greater length later on in the book.

Volunteer work establishes an individual as caring, sensitive, and sharing, and who is interested in helping others, and giving something back. It shows what kind of person you are, and is an indication of how you may function with others in the workplace. This is important to employers and contributes toward that competitive advantage. Every little bit helps.

If you are a college graduate, it is not necessary to list your high school. However, if it is a well-known school district, a specialty school for the industry being pursued, if you had strong achievements, or if you are pursuing a job in education, that prestige may be worth including. It cannot hurt!

Try to list references from internships or externships or other business experiences—they will be more believable than family or friends who may be viewed as obviously biased.

When using someone as a reference, be sure to secure that individual's permission beforehand, and advise them that a call from an employer may be forthcoming. It is the polite thing to do, and it avoids the embarrassment of an obviously unexpected call to a reference that makes you look less than thorough.

If your reference has been "tipped off," he or she may be inclined to put in a plug on your behalf—something along the line of: "I have been expecting your call, so-and-so told me about the interview with your company and is very excited about this possible opportunity. You're considering a very special person, in my opinion." Wow, before the conversation even begins a positive impression has already been made. All because of one simple heads-up phone call.

Do your best to keep your résumé to one page. People are busy, brevity is appreciated. However, if your particular situation necessitates a second page, use it. Be sure the second page is marked "page 2" and that your name and phone number appear at the top. Do not staple or paperclip. Leave it loose as you would the second page of a letter.

What to include (items marked with an asterisk should be listed in reverse chronological order, with the most recent one first):

—Name
—Phone numbers, e-mail and mailing addresses
—Objective (customized)
—Graduating college/high school* (optional)
—School achievements/awards*
—Previous employment/internship positions*
—Athletics/clubs/associations
—Skills
—Interests/volunteer work*
—"References upon request" (notify person[s] first)

This is the basic order for a "chronological" résumé. It will vary for a "functional" or "functional/chronological," and for priority purposes at different points in one's career. See the samples of the different types in Part 2.

—Chronological résumés: page 65
—Functional résumés: page 85
—Functional/chronological résumés: page 77

Appeal

Just as you may be more attracted to one ad versus others in a magazine because of an uncluttered, appealing layout, so too are employers attracted to résumés. Again, remember that great demands are placed on the individuals reading résumés. They are often pressed for time and can easily be turned off by a résumé that is too wordy or perceived as difficult to get through.

It has been stated that the decision to "pitch" or "consider" a résumé is usually made in ten to thirty seconds, so be very selective about what you submit.

In today's job market, the résumés of the two 2004 presidential candidates, George Bush and John Kerry, would probably fail the ten second rule—as in, employers know within ten seconds of seeing a résumé whether they will seek an interview.

Nobody thought that the two candidates were deadbeats. But they weren't bowled over either. Neither had a single internship—virtually required these days.

—*USA Today*, May 18, 2004

Do everything possible to gain the employer's full attention; be sure your résumé and cover letter are well organized, clear, and concisely written.

The following five points will help accomplish this goal:

—Customize the objective(s) to the specific interview
—Use clear, simple language
—Keep descriptions brief (bullet points are suggested)
—Check spelling/punctuation accuracy (have someone else read it)
—Include the person's title in letter address

Many things can be forgiven, but rarely an untruth. Stretching the truth or using a complete fabrication is a reflection of your character, personality, and credibility. If someone will lie once, they will do it again. Why hire that person? The truth somehow always surfaces. It is not worth the risk.

The reality is that a person looking at a résumé spends about thirty seconds on each one in the first cut. If you don't have at the top of the first page why you are the best, you don't stand a chance. I routinely deal with companies who receive more than three thousand résumés a day.

—Cheryl Dahle, *The New York Times*, April 17, 2005

Design

The initial reaction that an employer will experience toward your résumé will be visual. A clean, well-organized design will be well received. Contributing to this impression is the use of a typeface without serifs (a good one is Arial). Boldface/non-bold treatment is a very effective "highlighting" technique; examples are on pages 57–87.

To repeat, people in business are often short on time; a quick glance and scan of your résumé may be your only window of opportunity for attracting their interest and further drawing them into the details of your background. Résumé format should be pleasing to the eye.

Always use good quality paper for your résumé and cover letter—it will contribute to that initial impression. Use 24 lb. white or ivory stock, not color stationery. Here's what you want:

—Clean simple, orderly format
—Clear typeface
—Bold/non-bold for impact (headings, schools, companies, etc.)
—Good quality paper stock (not copier paper)

The one-picture-to-a-thousand words ratio unjustly downplays the importance of typestyles. Academics and marketers have long known that the choice of font in logos and advertising copy greatly influences legibility, memorability, and public perception of the brand.

—*Harvard Business Review*, April 2005

Action

Now that you have an attractively designed résumé, you should write a well-composed cover letter as well. Yes, a cover letter should *always* accompany your résumé. It is the bow on the package, so to speak, that creates the appropriate impression. Without it your effort is incomplete. Additionally, a cover letter allows you to briefly express yourself and gives the person reviewing your résumé a sample of your communication skills.

First, be sure your phone number(s) and e-mail address(es) are included in your cover letter; it may become separated from your résumé and you want to make it easy for people to contact you. Surprisingly this is often overlooked.

The use of e-mail, scanning, or fax to submit your résumé and cover letter is totally acceptable, and these are quick and efficient ways to communicate. In the fast-paced and competitive world that we live in, immediacy can be a significant advantage. Following up via first-class mail for that personal touch is always a good idea, where appropriate. The bonus is that your name passes before the employer an additional time. Also, the individual may have the opportunity to review your résumé in further detail and note something that was previously overlooked. Two impressions are better than one.

See pages 97–102 for cover letter samples.

Forwarding a Résumé

Until fairly recently, and before the miracle of technology, résumés were processed by first-class mail. Period. Today the options are far greater—and virtually instantaneous. However, the postal service is still the best method for quality impact. In the end, timing and availability will dictate the method used.

First-Class Mail

The primary advantage is the opportunity to showcase quality paper and the attractiveness of your résumé's layout and design without compromising them as you would when processing electronically. Another plus is your original signature on the accompanying cover letter.

The drawback to first-class is that your résumé will take several days to arrive at its destination. It can be further delayed in the mailroom or the person's inbox.

Scanning

A scanned résumé can be sent quickly and can be entered into the company's database. Frequently companies will program key words into the system that, when crossed with similar words on a given résumé, will create a match.

Since the scanner has the capability of identifying candidates with interests similar to the company's needs, it is important for multiple words and phrases that are synonymous to be built into the résumé text (i.e., stockbroker, investment executive, account executive, registered representative, etc.), so that whichever search phrase is used, *your* résumé will pop up. Give yourself every chance to be "discovered." (See a sample scanned résumé on page 91.)

Scanning Do's:

—Use standard clean-looking typefaces (fonts), such as Arial, Courier, or Times New Roman. Scanning software only recognizes certain fonts.

—Use 12-point type; it is easy to read.

—If your résumé goes to a second page (do try to avoid this) be sure your name and phone number and "page 2" appear at the top. Pages can become separated—make it easy for an employer or recruiter to locate you.

—The left margin should be "block" format or "flush left." The right margin should be "ragged" or "widowed," not "justified."

—Only use asterisks, not bullets, and spell out full symbols ("and," not "&")—neither bullets nor symbols will be "read" or transmitted.

—Use all capital letters for headings and names (not bold).

—Use white paper.

—For clarity use spacing before and after a slash or dash.

Scanning Don'ts:

—Do not underline, or use bold, italics, horizontal or vertical lines, boxes, borders, bullets, graphics, or symbols.

—Do not abbreviate.

—Do not use any typeface other than the standards: i.e. Arial, Courier, Times New Roman.

Electronic Résumé

E-mailing a résumé is a good option, if it is available to you. It is immediate and clean.

Since most businesses use Microsoft Word, there is a good chance that you will be able to forward your résumé in this format. If so, your exact résumé design and format should be received intact, as long as the sender's and receiver's versions of the software are compatible. Software is constantly being upgraded; if one version is less current than the other it may transmit differently or not at all.

Additionally do not use portable document format (PDF) or spreadsheets, and be sure to leave ¾" to 1" margins on top, bottom, and both sides.

The elements of designing a résumé for e-processing are discussed further in the scanning résumé section on page 88.

Web Résumé

This method offers the greatest flexibility by combining the benefits of first-class mail with the speed of the electronic résumé. Also, additional "spins" in the form of added pages, visuals, and sound can be included to make a résumé stand out from the crowd and create a further competitive edge. This method is particularly useful for creative positions where a portfolio and/or CD is important.

Fax

The résumé is quickly transmitted and received. However, it can be delayed in a central or individual's inbox. Also, it is printed on low-quality paper, with questionable reproduction quality.

If other options are available to you, faxing is probably the last choice.

Step 2
Obtaining an Interview

Options

Networking, networking, networking is your best source. Job opportunities come from many places—among the most productive are leads from family, friends, and fellow alumni. These are the people who know you best and may be most willing to extend themselves on your behalf. Talk to as many people as you can, let them know of your interests, ask if they can help or know someone who can. This is how informational interviews develop too—it is amazing how one thing leads to another.

Note that Internet sites (such as Monster.com) can certainly be effective, but can be overrun with résumés, especially in difficult economic times.

Only about 4 percent of people gain their jobs through the Internet. By contrast, 65 to 70 percent garner positions through informal contacts.
—International Association of Career Management Professionals

For college students, on-campus career days and college career service offices can be very useful and should be explored accordingly. These are readily available and require little effort. For the latter, remember that there are alumni who are very loyal to their colleges and who want to hire fellow graduates. Perhaps this is how they got their start, and they want to "pay back."

Of course, when you are looking for leads, it is important to provide as much specific information as possible. Simply saying that you are "looking for a job" is not sufficient. You cannot expect someone to call his or her contacts with only vague information. Not only is it meaningless, but it would be embarrassing and make them appear less than professional.

Finally, depending on the level of job that you are pursuing, executive recruiters and employment agencies can be good sources too.

This is the time to take out your pad and begin a personal assessment. Here you must be totally honest with yourself. You know yourself best. Start with your likes and dislikes. It is as important to know what you dislike as it is to know what you like. This is important! You will be working for a long time, so you might as well enjoy what you do. Many people do not—and dread getting up in the morning. Don't let yourself fall into that trap.

This list can be a gathering of hobbies and interests, previous involvement with college activities, volunteer work, internships/externships, or other business exposure. Also, do not overlook college courses that were of particular interest. When you network, knowing your interests, skills, likes, and dislikes will help others know best how they can help you.

Important: Whenever someone extends themselves on your behalf, it is only polite to thank them. Send a follow-up letter accordingly. It will be remembered because so few are aware or take the time to do so. It is good manners, smart business, and will serve to reinforce their decision to help you.

See page 109 for a sample.

We had a retail employer interviewing on campus. He said he expected every candidate to have set foot in that store.

—Warner Kister, Illinois Western University
The Bloomington Pantagraph, March 20, 2005

Know Yourself

What do you want? Where do you want to be? Know your temperament and personality: Where will you fit in best, a small or medium-size company or a large corporation?

In business it is important to be a team player. Selfishness and heroics won't cut it. Small and medium-size companies with fewer layers of management and less bureaucracy may suit you best. If that is a stretch, perhaps self-employment is best (where you make the rules).

If you are a patient and more diplomatic person who can deal with a more formal and, generally, a slower decision-making process, then you may do well in a larger corporation.

The key is to succeed and be happy. There is no right or wrong answer—only what is right for you. That's the bottom line!

Finally, are you willing to relocate or interested in doing so? This is a really important decision because it involves your emotional and personal life. Separation from family and friends can be tough and impact your job performance.

This is where it is really important to know yourself and what you want. For example, you may live in a wonderful city with year-round sun and surf, which is largely comprised of personal and small to medium-size businesses. But you realize you want a large corporation. In this case you must decide whether to relocate to where these types of companies are. If you choose to delay this move, and relocate at a later date, be aware that the job market will likely be more competitive (for entry/lower-level jobs) with the passing of subsequent graduating classes.

Have a plan and timetable. Know, to the best of your ability, where you want to be and when.

Do not be a procrastinator. Apply for jobs or internships early. Nothing will be gained by delaying—except competition with more applicants. Be aggressive and proactive. Create a competitive advantage!

Be Proactive

Your direct initiative with companies and organizations, expressing your interest and aspirations, is obviously key to being proactive—here that well-tailored résumé and cover letter can help separate you from the crowd.

If the job market is tight, exposure and networking through temporary employment agencies (temping) can pay off. Not only can you make contacts, but employers can experience the quality of your work, your attitude, personality, and work ethic first hand.

Let it be known that you would like to work for the company if a job becomes available. In doing so, you may have placed yourself in a position of contention. If the employer is happy with your work, why wouldn't they consider you? After all, you are already a proven quantity.

If you are determined to work for a given company and no temp jobs are available, consider offering your services for free—sort of an extended internship, same deal as temping—maybe something will open up. At the least, this approach can provide you with valuable experience while you continue to look for a job elsewhere. It also has the advantage of filling in what would otherwise be a gap on your résumé.

Traditionally, about 30 percent of temporary workers are hired full-time by the firms where they are working.

—American Staffing Association

Build and Maintain a Contact List

As you begin your job search, it is important to maintain good records. After meeting with a number of employers, conversations can begin to run together, and it may be difficult to recall who said what. A key to following up is accuracy—creating a database will spare you that confusion and embarrassment, while you build a contact list.

It is easy and takes little time. Make an entry immediately following a meeting or conversation while details are fresh in your mind, that way nothing will be omitted.

The following points should be covered:

—Company name and address
—Date contacted
—Who seen/spoken with
—Their responsibility
—Title of job being pursued
—Salary (if known or discussed)
—Interviewer's comments

—Suggested next steps
—Telephone/fax numbers
—E-mail address

Always ask for a business card. Not only is it proper protocol, but it will immediately provide half of the information you will need to maintain complete records. Having everything in one place will make your life easier too.

Also keep a copy of all correspondence for your file.

A small point with big consequences: Make business calls from a land line whenever possible—cell phones can have poor reception and make it difficult to clearly converse. This can test the patience of a potential employer—and kill an opportunity before it even begins.

Step 3
What to Do After Scheduling the Interview

Because job candidates generally do not think in terms of establishing a competitive edge, a letter preceding an interview will demonstrate your interest and your understanding of what it takes to get the job done.

This is the first step of your strategy. It is so easy it is almost sinful. The pre-interview confirmation letter does the following:

—Creates an initial impression
—Shows thoroughness
—Demonstrates an understanding of business
  procedures
—Indicates serious interest in the job
—Helps you stand out from competing applicants

This is something that most job applicants don't do—or forget to do—and can really separate you from the pack: *After* scheduling the interview but *before* the interview takes place, send a short letter expressing your appreciation for scheduling the interview, confirming the time and date, and expressing your interest. (See page 103 for a sample.) An employer who receives such a letter from you, and no one else, can only obtain a positive image of you. An initial competitive edge.

Consider the emotional aspects for a moment, and place yourself in the shoes of the interviewer. If all things are equal, and the interviewer is not previously acquainted with the candidates, a letter from one person and no one else creates an immediate advantage. It is an impressive effort that allows that individual to enter the interview one step ahead of the other applicants, and suggests the extra effort that they will bring to the workplace. In receiving a letter, the interviewer may feel a closer bond to that candidate—a good way to start an interview.

This is important to begin with since interviews are really about creating a favorable impression in a short period of time (generally fifteen to twenty minutes). This tactic gives you a running start.

Again, it is a good idea to attach a résumé even if one has already been forwarded. This gives the interviewer a chance to refamiliarize himself or herself with your background and accomplishments, and allows you to stand out a little more. Two impressions are better than one.

Your confirmation letter or e-mail should:
—Thank individual in advance for their time
—Confirm meeting date and time
—Express enthusiasm and interest in company and position
—Include your résumé

See page 103 for a sample confirmation letter.

Step 4
Preparing for the Interview

Have a Strategy

Just as a map will keep you on course for a car trip, an interview strategy designed to get you from point A to point B to point C, etc., will keep you on track and give you the best chance to succeed. Being prepared, knowing what to do and how to do it, will help illustrate your thoroughness, and allow you to stand out.

Since an average interview is approximately fifteen to twenty minutes, time can slip by quickly and important points that you may want to make can go unsaid.

Have a "game plan." Know where *you* want to go with an interview and how to work in key comments or points. Even though the interviewer is asking the questions, the responses are within your control. If your responses are organized and deliberate you will be able to work in the points that place you in the most favorable light, and further establish a competitive edge vis-à-vis someone who is merely responding in an unplanned random manner.

If a job candidate does not take the opportunity to respond to the employer's specific needs when they are expressed, another job seeker certainly will.

—*Chicago Sun-Times*, July 16, 2000

Types of Interviews

As part of your preparation, be aware that there are several types of interviews that you may encounter. While the dialogue of this book assumes a one-on-one situation, others could become part of the mix.

One-on-One Interview

The most common type of interview that is covered in detail throughout this book.

Telephone Interview

This method has become more widely used given personnel reductions and greater demand on interviewers' time. Initially screening applicants for proper qualifications: i.e., general intelligence, logical/rational skills, verbal skills, response, attitude, personality, etc., can quickly separate the "haves" from the "have-nots" and narrow the field.

Be concise. Phone interviews are generally fairly short, but a poor phone interview will likely kill your chances with that company. Review the questions in Part 4 (see page 117) in advance.

Group Interview

This is where a candidate will face off with more than one representative from the interviewing company, school district, etc., and questions will be asked, generally in a pre-rehearsed format.

This setting can obviously be very intimidating, and does not allow the advantage of establishing a rapport as you might in a one-on-one interview.

This type of interview can apply to any business and is at the discretion of the individual company. However, it is fairly common in education, or where a prospective employee will be required to give presentations, i.e., sales, advertising, or where other presentation skills are necessary.

Social Interview

This is generally over breakfast or lunch as a follow-up to the initial interview, and is where you are further evaluated, this time on social skills, etiquette, etc. This is discussed fully at the end of Step 5 (pages 43–44).

Become Informed

The first step toward being prepared is to be familiar with a given company (or nonprofit organization, government agency—whomever you're interviewing with): their strengths/difficulties, direction, and goals. Are these unique or common to that industry? If publicly traded, know the current stock price, fifty-two-week high/low, the name of the CEO, and any major recent news. (That is where the Internet comes in handy.)

If the company's products are sold through retail outlets, consider doing some market research; visit stores and speak with shoppers, sales-people, or the manager, ask what their opinions are of the products, how they compare to competition, what consumer comments are, and so on.

You can also prepare a questionnaire to record responses and verba-tims, then compile them on a summary page and use it appropriately during the interview or as a follow-up. It will show the employer that you went the next step to prepare, and that you took the time and showed interest to learn about their products.

Employers will be impressed with this type of effort, and you will likely have established a further competitive advantage because a very very low percentage of applicants will think or care to do this. See page 142 for a sample questionnaire.

Being prepared and armed with this type of information allows you to insert specific points into your responses to an interviewer's ques-tions. This enables you to speak knowledgeably and appear buttoned up, and allows you to set forth solid reasons for seeking employment.

Further, interviewers are impressed with individuals who have con-crete reasons for doing or wanting something. Nothing is better than a first-hand or hands-on experience that goes beyond simply wanting to secure a job in a certain industry.

Accordingly, if you were fortunate to have had an internship or ex-ternship with a company in the particular industry you seek, that is a wonderful base on which to build. It is a license to go beyond the ab-stract of "I *think* I want to enter this business" to "I *know* I want this business because . . ."

Become informed:
—Research the company/industry on the Internet
—Consider doing on-site research on the company's products or services
—Review company's annual report
—If publicly traded, know stock price/trends
—Have rationale for pursuing specific industry/company . . . incorporate academic/internship experiences

"The interview was over five minutes after it began.

"All I did was ask her what she could offer the magazine. All she could say was, 'Hmm-mmm, that's a toughie. I was more wanting to hear what you could do for me.'

"In an apparent attempt to redeem herself the candidate e-mailed a note elaborating on her qualifications. The note began: 'Besides the occasional hangover, here's what else I could bring into the office.'"

—Ron Donoho of *San Diego Magazine*, *The New York Times*, August 8, 2001

You can probably guess the outcome of this interview!

Know What the Interviewer Is Looking For

Be alert to what employers are looking for in a prospective candidate. If you organize your interview strategy around the five points employers typically look for, you will have taken a giant step toward projecting an image of quality and professionalism and ensuring a successful interview.

Understand that an employer is looking for a candidate who is:
—Attractive/presentable
—Articulate
—Enthusiastic
—Intelligent
—Informed

The very first impression an interviewer will have of you is visual, *not* verbal, as he or she greets you in the reception area or as you are escorted by an assistant to their office. Consciously or subconsciously that initial visual impression can have a disproportionate influence on the interviewer's overall assessment of you. So, be sure you are well attired and have good posture, confident body language, a pleasant smile, and a firm (not hard) handshake. This will be discussed in further detail later on.

Employers are obviously looking for people who will represent their company in an impressive manner. Hiring someone who is intelligent and well informed is an obvious goal—everyone wants to hire bright people—but it does not simply stop there. Being able to express yourself clearly and succinctly is key to interacting effectively in meetings and with clients, patients, or students. It is part of the package—there are plenty of smart people who lack this skill and whose advancement is limited accordingly.

Last, and certainly not least, is enthusiasm. This is the spark that makes the engine go—the ability to inject emotion, belief, and conviction into your thoughts and comments. It is the motivating factor that will help express your desire or ambition. Employers would rather hire someone that they have to rein in a little than someone who has to be pushed to be motivated.

A prestigious academic background does not guarantee eloquence. Older workplace professionals insist they are not ganging up on the younger generation but are simply fighting for verbal precision and intellectual clarity.

—*The New York Times*, February 17, 2002

Know What You Want to Say

Being prepared means not fumbling or hesitating: Know what you want to say, and how you want to say it.

Use a short greeting along the line of: "Good morning, Ms. [or Mr.]

Jones. Thank you for your time today, I have been looking forward to meeting with you." Short, sweet, and sets the tone.

Know that at some point you are going to be asked to describe your background, so be prepared to do so in an organized and concise manner—within sixty to ninety seconds. (If this sounds short, think about how much information is crammed into a fifteen-second television commercial.) This will give you enough time to provide that snapshot of who you are and set the stage for a give-and-take dialogue (as the interviewer probes with responding questions). This is what you want, the opportunity to expand further on your experiences and accomplishments without blabbing on in an initial one-way monologue that is almost certain to lose the interviewer's attention. Rehearse your background speech a few times—but not so much that it sounds forced or memorized.

Have a solid reason for pursuing a particular industry, and this specific company or organization within it. Tie into a previous employment, an internship or externship experience, or a course of study.

Be ready to insert remarks that are attractive to employers. For example, if you played a team sport or sang in a chorus, and the interviewer remarks about that activity, it is a perfect time to mention that you had fun, won a few games or competitions, but the most valuable lesson was gaining an appreciation for teamwork; something you feel will serve you well in business, because at the core of business success is teamwork. In doing so, you have demonstrated your understanding for professional life, and an ability to respond quickly. The interviewer cannot help but be impressed. This is simply a function of being prepared and opportunistic, and gaining a competitive edge.

To this end, it is a good idea to study your résumé and be prepared to respond to all experiences and activities that are listed, and which may surface as questions. (This also pertains to comments that are made in a cover letter.) For example:

Résumé Item	Response
athletics	teamwork
volunteering	caring, sensitivity, organization, and leadership skills
internship	knowledge of the industry
employment	description of responsibilities

A forty-minute monologue by a prospective employee is recalled. "He hardly came up for air." At the end the interviewer asked, "Do you have any questions?" The response: "No, I think you've answered all of my questions." But he hadn't asked any. This is not the kind of person you want around.

                              —David Moore, Sonostar Ventures, *The New York Times*, February 3, 2002

This interviewer was very patient—and probably very curious to see how long this person would babble on. Forty minutes—wow!

Anticipate the Interviewer's Questions

The interviewer will usually expand on the ensuing two-way dialogue with *traditional* questions such as: "Tell me about yourself," "Why do you want to work here?" "What are your strengths and weaknesses?" etc., that will give the interviewer further insights about you. Often the interviewer will also ask additional *behavioral* questions: "Do you like to win or hate to lose?" "Describe a problem you had, and how you solved it?" *Logic* questions are most appropriate for management consultants, engineers, etc., who are required to problem-solve in a more technical way. Samples of each are in Part 4:

—Traditional questions: pages 117–22
—Behavioral questions: pages 123–29
—Logic questions: pages 130–33

Remember, interviewing is all about questions and answers. You know they are coming, so be prepared.

This mentality is similar to studying well in advance for an exam and entering the classroom with a feeling of confidence, knowing you will do well—as opposed to cramming the night before, and being anxious and nervous because you are not properly prepared.

Most of us have done this at one time or another; it is not pleasant and we are almost doomed to fail.

Employers say that candidates who manage to land interviews are increasingly unprepared—sometimes woefully so—for the interviewing process. "Many can't provide details to probing questions."

> —Paige Soltano, Bozell, New York, *The New York Times,* August 8, 2001

There was an interviewee who was asked where she saw herself career-wise in five years. "How am I supposed to know?" she responded. "Isn't that your job?"

> —Jay Scherer, *Chicago Tribune,* July 8, 2002

As Tom Brokaw commented during his farewell remarks from *NBC Nightly News*: "It's not the questions that get us in trouble, it's the answers."

> —*NBC Nightly News*

Step 5
The Interview

The Initial Impression

Being an attractive, presentable candidate begins with attire and grooming. Dress to get the job. Employers look for individuals who will set forth a quality image of their company. So provide them with that image. Understand that unless you are pursuing a job in a creative industry where flamboyance is desirable, most businesses are of a conservative nature (education, medicine, law, banking, etc.) where corresponding attire is appropriate. They are not impressed with flashy bold colors and designs, short skirts or plunging necklines, but rather a smart and tasteful professional look.

I see young women all the time who wear little sun dresses with bra straps showing, along with fancy flip-flops. It's as if no one ever taught them how to look for a job.

—Paige Soltano, *The New York Times,* August 8, 2001

Remember, the people that you interview with are likely to be a number of years older than you, and they may not be impressed with young hip trends. So do not risk turning them off.

Dressing in conservative business attire does not mean that you have to be stuffy or boring, in fact you can look really sharp—consider some of the television news personalities; they are good examples that you may want to emulate.

So, for that initial impression:
>—Assume conservative corporate mentality
>—Dress for the occasion

—Dress for the masses
—Dress to get the job

Grooming Suggestions

The subject of appropriate grooming, attire, and common sense ties into earlier comments about marketing and packaging oneself for the purpose of introducing a new product into the marketplace. Here an element of packaging enters the equation and is a key component to that initial impression, the *visual* impression, that you will make.

Conservative business attire is important, however good common sense is also critical beyond the actual attire that is selected—and can be every bit as helpful or harmful. What does this mean?

Women

Attire: Women have more flexibility with color selection than men; just use good judgment and do not be too flashy. You cannot go wrong with blue, black, or gray. They can be "jazzed up" with tasteful accessories. Avoid sending the wrong message—be professional and classy in appearance. Be sure your skirt length and neckline are conservative. Of course, pants suits are totally acceptable. (Have the jacket buttoned upon entering interviewer's office.) And be sure to polish your shoes.

Jewelry: Keep it simple, not distracting or projecting a flashy image.

Perfume: Don't! Many people have allergic reactions to certain scents. This can be a distraction and potentially ruin an interview.

Fur: Do not wear it. You may be able to afford it, but perhaps the interviewer cannot. Do not create unnecessary jealousy or resentment. Encountering an animal-rights activist can also be a problem. You never know!

Hair and nails: Both should be neat and presentable, not flashy.

Stockings: Wear them. It projects a professional image.

Flirting: Don't. The reasons should be obvious.

Piercing: Limit to earrings.

Tattoos: Cover them up (if possible).

Don't forget to check your zipper! A young lady exited an interview thinking she had made a great impression. However, once outside she looked down to find her fly open with just the fluttering silk of her underwear between her and the world.

She didn't get the job.

—Linda Gilleran, Hewlett-Packard, *The New York Times*, February 3, 2002

Men

Attire: Blue or gray is best, it looks good and is versatile—different design and color ties can make these look like totally different suits. Err on the side of conservative. Wear black shoes (shined) and calf-length matching socks. While it may sound boring, a nice crisp white shirt is best for projecting a good corporate middle-of-the-road image, and is the most flexible. Enter the interviewer's office with your jacket buttoned and tie falling straight down (not off to the side). Do not make the mistake of wearing a blazer or sport jacket and slacks—it is not proper business attire. People will only take you as seriously as you take yourself. Of course there are exceptions to every rule. Pursuing a creative position may dictate less formal dress. A black T-shirt with a black jacket and appropriate slacks may be fine. Know your circumstances.

Grooming: To complete your professional impression, be sure your hair is neatly groomed, your nails are trimmed and clean, and you're clean shaven.

Piercing: Don't risk an unnecessary turn-off; remove any visible piercing (earrings, etc.). The interviewer is likely to be a number of years older than you, and may not share your taste. Besides, it lacks a professional image.

Tattoos: Cover up, if possible, for the same reasons as those explained in the section on piercing.

Cologne: Same as in the case of women, an allergic reaction or distaste for the scent can be distracting and kill an interview.

For women and men alike, do not be fooled by the "casual" environment of on-campus interviews. Approach these with a similar respect for proper attire as you would a "formal" office interview. Remember, first impressions are important. Interviewers take notes, and they will recall if you showed up in cut-offs or jeans and a T-shirt—or that you were appropriately attired.

On a personal note, in the early days of IBM, there was a dress code that required male employees to wear only white shirts. Unaware, I showed up for an interview wearing a blue shirt. The interview appeared to go well. At the very end, however, I was asked if I could "give up blue shirts." I said something ridiculous like, "Blue is my favorite color, why would I do that?"

Whether that was the reason I never heard from them again or not, I'll never know. However, I should have been better prepared, and was not. I never forgot that experience, and am constantly reminded of it whenever I hear IBM referred to by their nickname: "Big Blue." Go figure!

Creating a Great First Impression

Okay, you are well groomed and attired for obvious reasons, but not least of all is the fact that the very first impression an interviewer will have of you is visual; consciously or subconsciously initial impressions are lasting ones. We discussed this before, but it is worth mentioning again because it can be a deal breaker.

There is no substitute for a pleasant smile that radiates friendliness. It is amazing how something so simple can have such a strong and positive effect. Put that together with good posture, direct eye contact, a firm (not crushing) handshake, and confident body language, and you are off to a solid start.

If you are nervous and have sweaty palms do your best to discreetly wipe them as close to shaking hands as possible. Perhaps, carry your portfolio in your "shaking" hand and allow it to absorb perspiration, then switch it to the other hand moments before shaking hands. If you do this, leather or other absorbant material will work best.

Be on the safe side and address women as "Ms." Some may be offended by Miss or Mrs., and besides it can sometimes be difficult to know marital status. As slight as it may seem, there is no point in creating a possible negative reaction. If the interviewer prefers first names, they will direct you.

An initial impression can make or break you.

A senior-level candidate, who checked in with the receptionist, sat down, called his mother, and began "a loud conversation about how he had just gone to the dentist to have his gums trimmed." When a manager finally greeted him, the applicant said, "I'll be with you in a few minutes."

—Ann Maxfield, Project Solvers, *The New York Times,* February 3, 2002

Sometimes there simply is no explanation for stupidity!

Always bring additional résumés to the interview; you may be passed on to someone else that same day who does not have a copy. It is merely another example of being prepared. Be sure they are not creased or folded—it looks better.

To make a good initial impression, keep these points in mind:

—Punctuality (maximum ten minutes early)
—Nice attire
—Confident/polite tone of voice
—Direct eye contact
—Pleasant smile
—Firm (not hard) handshake
—Good posture/confident body language
—Address interviewer as "Ms." or "Mr."

Finally, if you saw an article in the press about the industry or company, it may be a good source for a question during the interview. Bring the actual article to the interview, not for the purpose of giving it to the interviewer, but as a visual aid. It will cast you in a good light and help toward establishing a greater competitive edge. Of course there is also the possibility that the individual did not see the article. In that case she or he may want to make a copy, and you have done them a favor. Additionally, bring a portfolio folder with pad and anything else appropriate to interview.

Arriving for the Interview

First, be sure your cell phone or beeper is off—the only thing more embarrassing than having one go off in the movies is during an interview.

When you enter the interviewer's office, demonstrate good manners and wait to be invited to be seated. Look confident by assuming good posture.

Since this is a business meeting and not a social occasion, sit with your legs uncrossed. Often men cross their legs and expose hairy calves above the top of their socks—not only does this project the wrong image, but it is unsightly. A natural position is holding your hands in your lap with your portfolio—it is a good look, as you are ready for your meeting and note-taking.

Yes, note-taking. There may be key points that will be important for follow-up purposes, and which can easily be forgotten. Recording them is a fail-safe precaution and, not least of all, illustrates your thoroughness and work habits. It may also flatter the interviewer because you felt what he or she said was important enough to write down. Winning at an interview is scoring points one at a time.

Finally, always appear calm and in control—try not to bounce your leg nervously, fidget, or rub your fingers—it will take away from the image you are attempting to project, and possibly distract the interviewer from concentrating on your comments rather than your motions. Remember, employers are more likely to hire an individual who they perceive as confident vis-à-vis someone who may easily be rattled or who is unsure of themselves.

> **Assuming good manners and appearance means that you:**
> —Turn off cell phone/beeper
> —Sit only when invited
> —Assume good posture

—Keep legs uncrossed
—Keep hands in lap with portfolio
—Appear calm, poised, and in control

Experts say job seekers should convey calm without appearing lethargic, and energetic without coming across as hyperkinetic.

—The New York Times, February 17, 2002

Employers' first impressions can be the difference between a good job and a goodbye.

—The Cincinnati Enquirer, May 19, 2003

The Initial Portion of the Interview

We know that the interviewer will initiate questions and determine the course your meeting will take. However, the way that you respond can have a big effect.

From the outset of the meeting, maintain as much control as possible. This can begin by initiating the opening greeting and showing that you are proactive and confident. This also places the burden of response on the shoulders of the interviewer, and possibly avoids a few awkward seconds of hesitation, as interviewee and interviewer wait for the other to begin the conversation.

You are now invited to sit, and, if appropriate, you can comment on an object in the interviewer's office, a photo or piece of art, the view—something that can be a graceful "icebreaker" after the initial greeting. It is also a chance for the interviewer to get a quick sense of your personality, grace, and conversation skills.

Following these pleasantries, the middle portion of the interview begins. As you saw, the first portion is likely to be very brief, but is critical for creating a first impression. Be the initiator . . . begin the conversation by expressing your appreciation for interviewer's time and interest. The responding pleasantry will likely be followed by an inquiry about your interests/background, etc. Prepare to launch into the middle portion of the interview.

The Middle Portion of the Interview: Evaluation Points

The middle portion of the interview is key—this is where your skills are evaluated insofar as your ability to express your thoughts, logic, and enthusiasm in a concise and organized manner.

This is how you will be measured, and it is where the interviewer will sit back, ask questions, and *listen*. As your comments evolve, your personality, emotions, and sense of humor will naturally surface—because that's who you are. Be yourself.

An increase in inappropriate or slipshod language in job interviews has been noted, mostly by individuals in their twenties. Talk peppered with the words "like," "you know," "totally," and "cool" annoy some interviewers so much that they automatically reject the job candidate.

—*The New York Times*, February 17, 2002

This is where being prepared really pays off. You know certain questions are coming and you have pre-rehearsed responses . . . this will help you to control the interview to the best of your ability, and to perhaps motivate the interviewer to ask follow-up questions that you also have a rehearsed response to. The "teamwork" or "why do you want to work in this industry" responses that were discussed earlier are good examples. Pages 117–33 in this book will help you cover the bases when it comes to interview questions.

Clearly described responses in a orderly and logical manner, delivered with enthusiasm, timely humor, and let's not forget that nice smile, will combine to determine your success.

The key points for interview evaluation are:
>   —Verbal skills
>   —Organization of thoughts
>   —Logic/reasoning
>   —Personality
>   —Temperament, emotion, sense of humor
>   —Level of interest/enthusiasm

The Middle Portion of Interview: Conversation

Remember, it is important to limit your background description to sixty to ninety seconds so that a two-way dialogue can evolve as the interviewer probes your background and asks questions. There is a fine line between being too wordy and too brief; do not do yourself a disservice by skimping, but do not cause the interviewer to tune out by being too verbose. Your objective is to create a give-and-take dialogue.

This is where you can expect to be asked questions similar to those discussed earlier. So, be sure to be well rehearsed and able to respond without hesitation. Here role playing can be very helpful toward building confidence and poise.

During the 2004 presidential debate, a citizen asked President Bush: "Please give three instances in which you came to realize you had made a wrong decision and what you did to correct it." The president couldn't come up with a single boo-boo.

—*The Boston Globe*

While it is an opportunity for the interviewer to see how you think and react, it is also an ideal opportunity for you to ask questions and learn about the company, and to be sure it is a good fit for *you*. If not you may be better off investing more time searching for the right job, rather than facing that inevitability six months or a year later. Be a good listener. Be patient. This is a good example of where less is more.

Let the interviewers do the bulk of the talking if possible (an eighty-twenty balance is ideal). This is your best chance to gather information. Take advantage of it. Also, do not attempt to interrupt, correct a comment, or show an attitude—it will not enhance the impression that you seek.

This is the best time to score some points—comments on teamwork and work ethics may fit naturally here.

However, do not initially risk turning off an employer by asking questions that pertain to salary, time off, vacations, office hours, etc.; it may be taken the wrong way. There will be ample time to do so assuming your interview goes well.

You are looking for an opportunity, a break, a foot in the door—be willing to do whatever it takes to get the job you want—even if it means accepting less money than you anticipated. While a few thousand dollars may seem like a lot of money now, it will not make a difference over the course of your career. Just focus on getting started.

If the question of salary is thrown into your lap, and you are uncertain what the job pays, a good response is: "My primary objective is to work for the XYZ Company; while money is important it is a secondary consideration—I am sure that I will be treated fairly."

If you were able to research the salary range you can begin by saying: "I understand that the industry is paying $00,000–$00,000 for this type of position. However, my primary objective is . . . [pick up balance of sentence from above paragraph]."

This provides an answer to the question, while also demonstrating where your first priority lies—working for that company!

Middle conversation should be:
- —A pre-rehearsed description of your:
    - –Background (college, etc.)
    - –Prior work experience (or internships)
    - –Goals/objectives
    - –Answer to "why" questions
- —Neither too wordy nor too brief (sixty to ninety seconds)
- —Give-and-take dialogue
    - –Two-way information gathering
    - –Opportunity to ask questions
    - –Opportunity to score "sales" points (teamwork/work ethic)

Most people have never taken the time to examine the components of the jobs they've had until asked in an interview. That's the wrong time to start a self-assessment.

—Larry Cinco, Management Recruiters,
The San Diego Union-Tribune, December 3, 2001

The Wrap-up

A frequently asked question and signal that the interview is nearing its end is: "Do you have any questions?" (or its equivalent). Being prepared with one or two questions is extremely important—it makes you look smart, interested, and not just like a run-of-the-mill candidate. It is the finishing touch on your interview. Without it your earlier efforts can be reduced, or worse, your lack of response could cost you the opportunity to remain in contention for that job.

Never respond to that question by saying something to the effect of: "No, you were very complete in your description, I cannot think of any questions to ask." That is a sign that you are not curious or prepared to ask a question at a moment when one is appropriate, and perhaps an indication for the lack of initiative that you will bring to the job. This may appear to be a minor point, but interviewing evaluation is a series of observations combined to arrive at a bottom-line conclusion.

Come prepared with five or six questions to ask so that you're sure to end up with one or two, since some of the questions may be answered during the interview.

Exit Formalities

When the interviewer says: "It has been nice meeting you," or "Someone will be in touch," or "Give me a call in a few days," you know the interview is over. Do not try to prolong the meeting—if you had a plan and were prepared, you should have been able to work in your points and ask questions.

A recent candidate stood up to thank the interviewer for her time and, assuming she was finished with her newspaper, proceeded to pull it out of her office wastebasket—along with the remains of coffee and breakfast, which spilled out all over the floor.

—*The New York Times*

So much for that interview.

You should be prepared with pre-rehearsed remarks that will allow you to exit the interview with the same grace and professionalism that you entered with. The points below will allow you to do this thoroughly and quickly.

—It will be obvious when interview is over. At that point:
  –Thank interviewer for his or her time
  –Express pleasure of meeting him or her
  –Restate interest in position
  –Ask: "What is the next step?" (if not previously stated)

Interview in a Restaurant

If an employer invites you to breakfast, lunch, or dinner, it is a signal that you are now a serious candidate. But be cautioned, there is no such thing as a "free lunch." Yes, this is a test—to see how you handle yourself in a social situation and what can be expected when you interface with colleagues or clients. So, once again be prepared and much of the stress will be removed.

—As with any interview, always wear appropriate business attire, and be well groomed.
—Arrive at the restaurant first. Wait for your host to arrive before being seated. Once seated, place the napkin on your lap immediately.
—You will most likely be asked for your drink and lunch order first. Never order alcohol, only a soft drink or iced tea—regardless of what your host orders.

During her tenure as a training manager for Bank of America, Brooke Hodges deliberately took job candidates to lunch and watched.

Did the men pull out chairs for women? Did the candidates say "please" and "thank you"? Did they put their napkins on their laps? Did they wait for everyone to be served before eating?

—For lunch, only order an entrée. If your host orders a first course and asks if you would like one too, politely decline; the less food to deal with, the better. You are not there to eat, but rather converse—you do not want to be "obligated" to eat all that you order.

—Order simple food that is easy to cut and chew, nothing that is sloppy or requires work, such as shellfish, finger food, steak, pasta, etc. A salad is always safe—and you can ask that it be chopped before it is brought to the table. This allows you to maintain maximum control.

—If you have bread, tear off a small piece with your fingers and then put it in your mouth. Never tear a chunk off with your teeth. Do not gulp your drink.

—The drinking glasses are on the right side of the dish, bread plate on the left. Expect the waiter to serve from your left side and remove from the right.

—When you complete your meal, place the knife and fork at the four o'clock position on the plate.

—Decline dessert and coffee. If your host does not order either, he is then stuck waiting for you to be served and to complete your meal. He or she may be pressed for time and this will be extremely awkward for you. Of course, if your host says, "I'm having coffee, would you like some too?" it is then okay to do so. If you prefer tea, say so.

—If your host thanks you for joining him or her for lunch, again express your appreciation and thanks for lunch, and emphasize your enthusiasm and determination for wanting the job. Also, be sure to get follow-up directions.

—Upon leaving the table, push in your chair, and precede your host out of the restaurant. Shake hands outside the restaurant. Exchange pleasantries and whatever else is appropriate from your luncheon conversation. (Remember to thank your host again for lunch.) Do not attempt to extend the conversation. Lunch is over.

Now the time has come for you to compose a follow-up letter and, ideally, have it received that day or the next morning.

Hopefully, your good manners, etiquette, and poise are another plus in the competitive edge column—and have inched you further toward a job offer. It all adds up!

"You're not going to impress someone by knowing good table manners, but you run the risk of turning them off if you don't have good table manners," says Carol Haislip, International School of Protocol.

—*The Baltimore Sun*, March 16, 2005

Step 6
Post-Interview Follow-up

Initial Follow-up Letter

A follow-up letter is *very* important, and it is amazing how many people do not take the time to write, or are unaware of this protocol. In a way, it is also an opportunity to "extend the interview" by carefully making certain follow-up points.

First, it is good manners to thank someone for their time; and good manners, taste, and judgment are really important. People tend to gravitate to those they *like* to do business with rather than people they *have* to do business with. Secondly, it allows you to sell yourself further by demonstrating your professionalism, understanding of business procedures, communication skills, and your continued enthusiasm for the job. Prospective employers are looking for that spark, the energy indicating that you *really want* this position. It should be sent the same day as the interview, or within twenty-four hours.

The points to cover are similar to the exit formalities. However, the middle part of your letter should discuss items from the interview itself, and should reinforce your capabilities for the job requirements that the employer seeks.

It is the icing on the cake—and interviewers like dessert!

Your follow-up letter should include:
> —Thank-you for time
> —Expression of interest/enthusiasm
> —Why you are a good fit
> —What you can contribute
> —References to point(s) discussed during interview
> —Restatement of follow-up agreement

See page 107 for a sample follow-up letter.

Recruitment managers emphasize the "soft skills." These include written and oral communications, the ability to ask the right questions, and a commitment to continuous improvement.

—*USA Today*, April 22, 2004

Second Follow-up Letter

Perhaps you were one of the applicants to interview early in the process and a decision will not be made for two or three weeks. If that is the case, or if a reasonable amount of time has passed and nothing further has transpired, it is important to keep the ball moving and not be forgotten or give the impression that you are not interested in the job.

So, be creative. A second letter is an excellent way to continue the communication process and maintain momentum. In short, it's an invisible excuse to communicate. This can be done about halfway between your initial interview and when you understand a decision will be made.

However, be sure that the content of your letter is solid and not simply fluff. Perhaps make comments about an article related to that industry, the company itself, or an expansion of a point discussed in your interview. This can also be an ideal time to report on that "research field trip" to stores and your conversations with shoppers, salespeople, and managers. The survey results are an excellent subject of discussion here.

Remember, it is important to separate yourself from the pack, and the majority of applicants that you are competing with will not do this. Bingo, another plus for you.

Second follow-up letter creates a chance to:
> —Communicate
> —Stand out
> —Reference item discussing company/industry or a
>   point from meeting
> —Express continued interest/enthusiasm

See page 108 for a sample letter and page 142 for a sample questionnaire.

Job Offer Follow-up Letter

After you receive that eagerly awaited job offer, and your pulse has returned to normal, do one last thing: write an individual thank-you letter to each person you interviewed with.

Thank each one for their support and confidence, and for the opportunity to join them and work together (synonym for "teamwork").

This touch will reinforce their decision to hire you, demonstrate your professionalism—and yes, score another plus for you. Again, it is surprising that most people miss this opportunity, this finishing touch.

Send *individual* letters because letters are often circulated to other people who are involved with the interview process. The letter that you sent to one person may be terrific, so much so that it is passed on to someone else (who may have their own letter from you) perhaps with a comment along the line of: "Nice follow-up—looks like a good hire." If person B reviews the letter and notes that it is exactly the same as the one she or he received, or maybe only the first paragraph is different, the implication is that you are taking a shortcut, or did not think that the person was important enough to receive an individual letter. After all your hard work—scheduling the appointment, preparing, traveling to and from the interview, the interview itself, following up, and going through the anxiety of waiting for a decision—do not risk planting a negative seed. So make each letter different!

See page 110 for a sample letter.

A candidate for a job at a major magazine wrote thank-you notes to both editors who had interviewed her. But her carelessness did her in; she forgot to insert the name of one of the editors in her form letter.

"On one letter she got the name right. The other letter was written to Dear Blah Blah. The woman who got the Blah Blah was really insulted."

—Dana Cowin of *Food & Wine* magazine, *The New York Times,* August 3, 2002

Job Rejection Follow-up Letter

If you do not get the job it may not be because you failed somehow. Perhaps there was only one job opening and you were a strong runner-up. Maybe the chosen candidate will turn out to be a disappointment. If so, you may be in a good position to be considered as their replacement. Another position may open up. Who knows? I can speak first hand to this situation. One time the interview process was narrowed down to two candidates. Both were impressive, but only one position was available. About a month later a similar job opened up in another department, I recommended the runner-up, and she subsequently got the job. Strange things happen!

With those possibilities in mind, a follow-up letter expressing your thanks for the interviewer's time and consideration, your continued interest in the company, a request for future consideration, etc., could pay off down the line.

You never know what is going to happen, or where or when paths will cross—especially with the frequency that people change jobs. The person that you interviewed with today can be elsewhere tomorrow. Keep the ball rolling, make things happen—in order to do so you must be alert, opportunistic, and proactive. Networking produces wonderful results in unexpected ways. So take a few minutes to finish the job right. You may profit in the end.

See page 112 for a sample letter.

Letter for Withdrawal or Declining an Offer

For whatever the reason may be, it is very important to handle either of these situations with great tact and diplomacy—*never* burn bridges or create resentment. The world has become a very small place, and each given industry even smaller.

Paths cross, people know other people you may know, and word quickly gets around about an individual who acts in poor taste. Your reputation is all that you have. It is difficult and time consuming to establish a good one, but it can be destroyed in moments.

Handle these types of situations carefully. Be gracious, humble, and sincere. Offer a truthful explanation and ask for their understanding.

The individual may have been in a similar situation at one time in his or her career and be totally understanding. You are not the first nor will you be the last to withdraw or decline a job, it happens. Just handle it with good taste and judgment.

See pages 113–14 for sample letters.

Who to Copy on Letters

As you move through the interview process at a given company, it is important to keep everyone in the loop so that they can stay abreast of your progress.

This can be easily done by open copying each person that you previously saw on the letter to the person you most currently interviewed with. This continues to demonstrate your understanding of sound business procedures and your communication skills. Further, it can create positive "buzz" as inquiries and comments are exchanged among the people you have seen, and who collectively decide who gets hired. Look upon it as part of your planned strategy. This is often overlooked by interviewees, and can result in another plus for you. The competitive advantage expands in your favor.

Copy the other people by inserting "cc:" and their names (flush left and a couple of spaces below your signature—see pages 97–98).

By the way, "cc" stands for "carbon copy," a relic of the pre-photocopier days when document copies had to be typed on carbon paper!

Never give the impression to a person that you interviewed with earlier that they are no longer important: "Sweat the small stuff."

A stained carpet in the office or a burned-out reading light on an airplane may seem inconsequential. But when management ignores such trivial irritations, it is effectively telling employees or customers that they don't matter.

—*Harvard Business Review*, April 2005

Summary

At this point you should feel comfortable about the interview process by knowing *what to expect* and *how to react*.

The following sections go to the next level and offer sample résumés, letters, interview questions, and a research questionnaire that will thoroughly prepare you for those aspects and allow you to be a well-rounded candidate.

So, be prepared. Enter the interview with a game plan, a strategy that will take you from A–Z, and hopefully on to the payroll! Good luck, and if you follow everything in this book, you should increase your potential for a successful interview.

Part 2

Sample Résumés

One of the editorial goals of *Don't Blow the Interview* has been to present the contents of this book in a clear and empathic manner. To that end, and with special regard to sample résumés, a "building block" approach has been applied.

This has been accomplished by tracking one individual, beginning with the internship job search in the freshman year of college, and continuing through the various stages of their business career. This technique allows the reader to see how a résumé changes, what is added and deleted, etc.

Since this individual's background is constant on the one hand, but steadily evolving on the other, the reader should be able to adapt similar résumé adjustments to the particular circumstances at a given point in their own career.

Note that for space reasons, many of the résumés are shown over two pages—unless specifically noted in the text, in "real life" they would be limited to one page in length.

Types of Résumés

There are three types of résumés that are typically used.

Chronological

The most commonly used style, especially for students seeking internships, graduating students, recent graduates seeking their first jobs, or for those who are relatively new to the work force with a limited amount of experience. (Examples on pages 57, 59, 61, 65, and 69.)

Functional

Appropriate for those with more extensive credentials who wish to elaborate on specific experiences, qualifications, and/or accomplishments. Also used to minimize attention to periods of unemployment. (Example on page 85.)

Chronological/Functional

A middle ground between a "chronological" and "functional" résumé allows job seekers to list job experiences in a more abbreviated chronological order, while zeroing in on specific experiences, accomplishments, and/or skills in another section.

(The résumés on pages 73, 79, and 81 are mostly chronological with slight functional elements. Page 77 contains a complete example of the combined "chronological/functional" format.)

Résumé Checklist

What to include:
- ☐ Phone numbers, e-mail and mailing addresses
- ☐ Objective (customized)
- ☐ Graduating college (or high school)
- ☐ Honors/awards
- ☐ Employment/internship positions
- ☐ Other activities, clubs, associations, volunteer work
- ☐ Interests
- ☐ Phrase "References upon request"

Appeal:
- ☐ Clear simple language
- ☐ Brief descriptions
- ☐ Be truthful
- ☐ Check spelling/punctuation

Design:
- ☐ Pleasing to the eye
- ☐ Clean, simple, orderly
- ☐ Clean typeface (i.e., Arial, Times New Roman)
- ☐ Use bold to make headings, school/company names stand out
- ☐ 20–24 lb. white/off-white stationery (not copier or color stock)
- ☐ 10–12 point type size

Action:
- ☐ Cover letter should always accompany résumé
- ☐ Include person's title in address
- ☐ Minimize use of the word "I"

Suggested action words for objective statement:
- ☐ apply
- ☐ broaden
- ☐ expand
- ☐ obtain
- ☐ pursue
- ☐ secure
- ☐ seek

Résumé Comments: Building Block #1
College Freshman Seeking Internship

At this early age in one's life, it is understandable and expected that a résumé will be modest. Beyond high school, which is standard for all applicants, other activities are probably limited to summer jobs. These will help to fill out the résumé and show that you have been active and engaged.

Note the inviting appearance of this résumé. The layout is orderly and well spaced. The typeface is clean and easy to read. No clutter.

Use 12-point type if you have room. In cases where you need to fit more on a page, reduce the typeface to 11-point.

Format: Chronological résumé works here—it clearly demonstrates that the individual worked and did not just goof the summers away.

Address: Remember, make it easy to be contacted, provide temporary and permanent contact information, including phone numbers.

Objective: Shows a win-win understanding, a benefit to the employer in exchange for an opportunity to learn. This individual is interested in learning and making a contribution.

Work Experience: Summer jobs are summer jobs; do not exaggerate about responsibilities.

College Activity: During this infancy stage, early involvement with college activities, student government, etc. will work in one's favor and help to form a picture of who that person is. This, in addition to high school summer jobs, gets the ball rolling.

Sample Résumé: Building Block #1
College Freshman Seeking Internship

Tracy Richards

Temporary Address
Lafayette College
Westville, PA 12345
610-555-0123
richardst@lafyt.edu

Permanent Address
761 Brewster Road
St. Paul, NY 12345
914-555-0123
richardst@mindnet.com

Objective: To pursue a summer internship in the financial services business for the purpose of experiencing the industry environment, while contributing to office productivity.

Education:
Lafayette College, Westville, PA   9/98–Present
   *Liberal Arts/English Major
   *GPA 3.2
St. Paul High School, St. Paul, NY   9/94–6/98

Work Experience:
St. Paul Recreation Department, St. Paul, NY summer 1998
Summer camp counselor for six-year-old girls
   *Supervised their activities and well-being
   *Read stories during rest period
   *Maintained attendance records

Assistant camp counselor for six-year-old girls   summer 1997
   *Assisted counselor with above functions

Activities:
*Tutored homeless children, White Plains, NY   1996–1998
*Volunteer, White Plains Hospital   1995–1998
*St. Paul High School: lacrosse, field hockey,   1994–1998
   chorus

College Activity:
Lafayette College Student Government   9/98–Present
   *Member of Freshman Activities Committee

Skills: Microsoft Word, PowerPoint, Excel, Internet

Interests: Tutoring disadvantaged children, reading, sports

REFERENCES UPON REQUEST

Résumé Comments: Building Block #2
College Sophomore Seeking Internship

The résumé is still modest, but now includes an initial internship experience during the summer of the freshman year.

Making the leap into the business world demonstrates ambition, curiosity, and an interest in learning and exploring. This begins to build a positive image and will certainly help when applying for a second internship.

Format: Chronological format is still appropriate.

Objective: Note that the job objective has been adjusted to reflect a change from "finance" to "advertising media." The balance of the statement remains unchanged. No need to reinvent the wheel. This résumé is going to an entirely different business and group of people.

Education: Freshman year GPA is added (only if 3.0+). Note GPA is moved up a line (compared with previous résumé) to help keep résumé to one page. Tinkering of this nature is ongoing.

Business Experience: Freshman internship is added. This begins to fill out the résumé.

College Activities: Additionally, this individual shows a further interest in becoming involved with new experiences in student government and on the school newspaper. Intramural sports implies a well-rounded person with a wide range of interests.

Sample Résumé: Building Block #2
College Sophomore Seeking Internship

Tracy Richards

Temporary Address
Lafayette College
Westville, PA 12345
610-555-0123
richardst@lafyt.edu

Permanent Address
761 Brewster Road
St. Paul, NY 12345
914-555-0123
richardst@mindnet.com

Objective: To pursue a summer internship in the advertising media business for the purpose of experiencing industry environment, while contributing to office productivity.

Education:	**Lafayette College,** Westville, PA	9/98–Present
	*Liberal Arts/English Major/GPA 3.4	
	St. Paul High School, St. Paul, NY	9/94–6/98

Business Experience:

Prudential Securities, Inc. New York, NY — summer 1999
Intern to portfolio managers. Assisted with:
* Research and analysis for corporate 10Q, 10K, and annual reports
* Organization/preparation of client profit and loss and asset allocation statements
* Reviewed and adjusted client spreadsheets

St. Paul Recreation Department, St. Paul, NY — summer 1998
* Summer camp counselor for six-year-old girls
* Supervised their activities and well-being
* Read stories during rest periods
* Maintained attendance records

Assistant camp counselor for six-year-old girls — summer 1997
* Assisted counselor with above functions

College Activities:
* Lafayette College Student Government — 9/98–Present
  Member of Student Activities Committee
* Lafayette College newspaper staff writer — 9/98–Present
* Intramural sports — 9/98–Present

Other Activities:
* Tutored homeless children, White Plains, NY — 1996–1998
* Volunteer, White Plains Hospital — 1995–1998
* St. Paul High School: lacrosse, field hockey, chorus — 1994–1998

Skills: Microsoft Word, Power Point, Excel, Internet

Interests: Tutoring disadvantaged children, reading, sports

REFERENCES UPON REQUEST

Résumé Comments: Building Block #3
College Junior Seeking Internship

The résumé begins to show substance with back-to-back summer internships. It is premature to delete pre-college activities. Therefore a second page is required as new experiences are added. The résumé will revert back to one page shortly, when "teen" jobs and activities are deleted.

Internships are about exploring and sampling different businesses. Take advantage of the opportunity, it is a limited time frame. While they are generally unpaid positions, do not be turned off. Look at them as an extension of your education.

Here type size can be increased to 12 point to help fill out the page as the résumé expands to two pages.

Format: Chronological format continues. Note résumé is extended to a second page. This is okay since the additions are of substance. Nothing has been deleted since we are still in the building stage.

Objective: Once again, the objective only changes insofar as the industry that is being pursued (from "advertising media" to "television"). There is no reason to rewrite the entire statement.

Education: As résumé goes to two pages, GPA is moved to a separate line to help fill out the page.

Business Experience: Second internship is added.

(continued)

Sample Résumé: Building Block #3
College Junior Seeking Internship

Tracy Richards

Temporary Address
Lafayette College
Westville, PA 12345
610-555-0123
richardst@lafyt.edu

Permanent Address
761 Brewster Road
St. Paul, NY 12345
914-555-0123
richardst@mindnet.com

Objective: To pursue a summer internship in the television industry for the purpose of experiencing the environment, while contributing to office productivity.

Education:

Lafayette College, Westville, PA	9/98–Present
*Liberal Arts/English Major	
*GPA 3.4	
St. Paul High School, St. Paul, NY	9/94–6/98

Business Experience:

Horizon Media, New York, NY   summer 2000
Intern to Account Management Groups for:
A&E Network, History Channel, GEICO
  *Included in media/marketing strategy meetings
  *Researched and analyzed competitive media spending
  *Prepared reconciliation spreadsheets for invoicing
  *Plotted flow charts for media activity and spending
  *Performed agency trafficking functions

Prudential Securities, Inc., New York, NY   summer 1999
Intern to portfolio managers. Assisted with:
  *Research and analysis for corporate 10Q,
   10K, and annual reports
  *Organization/preparation of client profit
   and loss and asset allocation statements
  *Reviewed and adjusted client spreadsheets

St. Paul Recreation Department, St. Paul, NY   summer 1998
Summer camp counselor for six-year-old girls
  *Supervised their activities and well-being
  *Read stories during rest periods
  *Maintained attendance records

Assistant camp counselor for six-year-old girls   summer 1997
  *Assisted counselor with above functions

(continued)

Résumé Comments: Building Block #3
College Junior Seeking Internship
(*Page 2 of Résumé Comments*)

Contact Information: Name and phone numbers are included on page 2. As previously mentioned, things happen, pages can become separated. Make it easy to be located.

College Activities: Promotion from staff writer is indicated. This is important since it shows growth.

Sample Résumé: Building Block #3
College Junior Seeking Internship
(Page 2 of Sample Résumé)

Tracy Richards

610-555-0123 temporary
914-555-0123 permanent

College Activities:	*Lafayette College Student Government Member of Student Activities Committee	9/98–Present
	*Lafayette College Newspaper	
	*Sports Editor	9/99–Present
	*Staff Writer	9/98–5/99
Other Activities:	*Tutored homeless children, White Plains, NY	1996–1998
	*Volunteer, White Plains Hospital	1995–1998
	*St. Paul High School: lacrosse, field hockey, chorus	1994–1998
Skills:	Microsoft Word, PowerPoint, Excel, Internet	
Interests:	Tutoring the disadvantaged, reading, sports	

REFERENCES UPON REQUEST

Résumé Comments: Building Block #4
College Senior Preparing for Full-Time Job Search

Our sample résumé writer has grown nicely through the years, thanks to a solid "game plan," forward thinking, and the knowledge of what it takes to become a saleable and attractive job candidate.

The type size can be reduced to 10-point. This, along with deletions, will keep the résumé to one page (though in this book, it is shown on two).

Format: Again, the chronological format continues.

Objective: For the first time the objective completely changes to reflect a specific industry and career path.

Education: Dean's list honor is added as GPA goes from 3.4 to 3.5.

Delete high school, if appropriate. See comment in "business experience" below.

Business Experience: A third internship is added. With three internships headlining the résumé, it is now appropriate to delete references to high school, "teen" jobs, activities, etc., unless they contribute in some way to the effectiveness and impression of your résumé. For example:

—Graduating from a "brand name" or prestigious high school.
—If an individual lacks multiple internships, these may be needed to help fill out a résumé.
—If "teen" jobs/activities relate to the chosen career path.

(continued)

Sample Résumé: Building Block #4
College Senior Preparing for Full-Time Job Search

Tracy Richards

College Address	**Permanent Address**
Lafayette College	761 Brewster Road
Westville, PA 12345	St. Paul, NY 12345
610-555-0123	914-555-0123
richardst@lafyt.edu	richardst@mindnet.com

Objective: To secure an entry-level position in the advertising agency business with specific focus on media planning and buying. This decision is a result of a fulfilling internship experience.

Education: **Lafayette College**, Westville, PA   9/98–Present
  *Bachelor of Arts, English
  *Dean's List/GPA 3.5

Business Experience: **The A&E Network,** New York, NY   summer 2001
Intern to creative team that produced promotional television spots
  *Screened upcoming A&E shows for the purpose of developing promotional copy
  *Viewed promotions for presentation clarity
  *Researched Internet for events A&E might consider for program development
  *Completed supplementary assignments from the marketing and advertising directors

Horizon Media, New York, NY   summer 2000
Intern to Account Management Groups for:
A&E Network, History Channel, GEICO
  *Included in media/marketing brainstorming meetings
  *Prepared reconciliation spreadsheets for client invoicing
  *Plotted flow charts for media activity and spending
  *Performed agency trafficking functions

Résumé Comments: Building Block #4
College Senior Preparing for Full-Time Job Search
(*Page 2 of Résumé Comments*)

College Activities: Note promotion to assistant managing editor. This continues to show growth. But now the important element of leadership also emerges. The position at the newspaper now takes top billing. Student government is listed second.

Other Activities: The only "teen" job remaining is tutoring oriented. This continues to show an on-going track record for character. Also, a similar volunteer activity during college is added.

Sample Résumé: Building Block #4
College Senior Preparing for Full-Time Job Search
(*Page 2 of Sample Résumé*)

Prudential Securities, Inc., New York, NY   summer 1999
Intern to portfolio managers. Assisted with:
  *Research/analysis for corporate 10Q, 10K,
  and annual reports
  *Organization/preparation of client profit
  and loss and asset allocation statements
  *Reviewed and adjusted client spreadsheets

College Activities: Lafayette College Newspaper   9/98–Present
*Currently serving as assistant managing editor
  Previously held sports editor and staff
  writer positions

Lafayette College Student Government   9/98–Present
  *Member Student Activities Committee

Other Activities: "Kids in the Community" tutor, Westville, PA   1998–Present
Tutored homeless children, White Plains, NY   1996–1998

Skills: Microsoft Word, PowerPoint, Excel, Internet

Interests: Tutoring the disadvantaged, reading, sports

REFERENCES UPON REQUEST

Résumé Comments: Building Block #5
College Graduate Pursuing First Full-Time Job

Now is the time to make minor adjustments in the résumé to reflect post-college status.

Note the subtle distinctions between being a "college senior preparing for a first full-time job," and a "college graduate pursuing a first full-time job."

Format: Still a chronological format.

Address: The "temporary" address and phone number have been removed. Only the "permanent" information remains. Restructure the heading so that the name, address, etc., is centered at the top. The name should stand alone on line one.

Objective: If career choice has changed (from pre-graduate statement) restructure objective statement. (In this example it remains unchanged.)

Education: High school can be deleted unless one of the points discussed on the previous résumé ("College senior preparing for first full-time job") prevails.

Dates: Change college attendance from "present" to the month and year graduated. Same for "college activities" and "other activities."

Business Experience: High school and teen jobs should be deleted unless beneficial toward the field being pursued.

Sample Résumé: Building Block #5
College Graduate Pursuing First Full-Time Job

Tracy Richards

761 Brewster Road
St. Paul, NY 12345
914-555-0123/richardst@mindnet.com

Objective: To secure an entry-level position in the advertising agency business with specific focus on media planning and buying. This decision is a result of a fulfilling internship experience.

Education: **Lafayette College**, Westville, PA   9/98–5/02
*Bachelor of Arts, English
*Dean's List/GPA 3.5

Business Experience: **The A&E Network**, New York, NY   summer 2001
Intern to creative team that produced promotional television spots
*Screened upcoming A&E shows for the purpose of developing promotional copy
*Viewed promotions for presentation clarity
*Researched Internet for events A&E might consider for program development
*Completed supplementary assignments from the marketing and advertising directors

Horizon Media, New York, NY   summer 2000
Intern to Account Management Groups for:
A&E Network, History Channel, GEICO
*Included in media/marketing brainstorming meetings
*Researched and analyzed competitive media spending
*Prepared reconciliation spreadsheets for client invoicing
*Plotted flow charts for media activity and spending
*Performed agency trafficking functions

Sample Résumé: Building Block #5
College Graduate Pursuing First Full-Time Job
(*Page 2 of Sample Résumé*)

| | **Prudential Securities, Inc.**, New York, NY | summer 1999 |

Prudential Securities, Inc., New York, NY   summer 1999
Intern to portfolio managers. Assisted with:
  *Research and analysis for corporate 10Q,
   10K, and annual reports
  *Organization/preparation of client profit and
   loss and asset allocation statements
  *Reviewed and adjusted client spreadsheets

College   Lafayette College Newspaper   9/98–5/02
Activities: *Ultimately served as assistant managing editor
                       Previously held sports editor and staff writer
                       positions

                       Lafayette College Student Government   9/98–5/02
                        *Member of Student Activities Committee

Other   "Kids in the Community" tutor, Westville, PA   1998–5/02
Activities: Tutored homeless children, White Plains, NY   1996–1998

Skills: Microsoft Word, PowerPoint, Excel, Internet

Interests: Tutoring the disadvantaged, reading, sports

REFERENCES UPON REQUEST

Résumé Comments: Building Block #6
Master's Degree Individual Pursuing Next Job

Important additions from the previous "college graduate pursuing full-time job" résumé are reflected here.

The added credentials of full-time business experience and a master's degree are wonderful entrées to that next job move.

"Other Activities" have been deleted—they will have little importance at this point.

Format: The résumé moves slightly towards the "chronological/ functional" format with the addition of "qualifications" section.

Objective: Changes indicate previous business and graduate school experiences (that are benefits to employer), and the new position being pursued.

At this point it is appropriate to state the specific name of the company of interest.

Qualifications: Now that business exposure has been achieved, key experiences and responsibilities are listed in this section.

Business Experience: Add first full-time job. Final employment date is changed from "present" to actual month and year.

(continued)

Sample Résumé: Building Block #6
Master's Degree Individual Pursuing Next Job

Tracy Richards

900 West 8 Street
New York, NY 12345
212-555-0123 /richardst@mindnet.com

Objective: To apply my previous experience and knowledge in advertising media and graduate school toward an assistant brand manager position at (name of company).

Qualifications:
* Master of Business Administration degree
  * Thorough understanding of interaction between advertising agency and client
  * Exposure to brand management at client meetings
  * Familiarity with the relationship between marketing, media, product design, distribution, and the role that advertising plays to promote and facilitate consumer awareness and demand
  * Creative, efficient, organized worker
  * Promoted from assistant media planner to media planner to senior media planner within 18 months

Business Experience: **Yates Advertising,** New York, NY   9/02–6/04
Senior Media Planner
  * Media planning/buying responsibilities for $7 million print budget for Sparkle mouthwash
  * Presented media proposals to advertising agency and client management
  * Supervised assistant and media planner
  * Interacted with magazine publishers, negotiated rates and value-added packages

Other Experience: **The A&E Network,** New York, NY   summer 2001
  Intern to creative team that produced promotional television spots
Horizon Media, New York, NY   summer 2000
  Intern to Account Management Groups for: A&E Network, History Channel, and GEICO

Résumé Comments: Building Block #6
Master's Degree Individual Pursuing Next Job
(*Page 2 of Résumé Comments*)

Education: Graduate school name/date is added. Note that the "education" section has been moved to the lower portion of the résumé. As job experience expands, it becomes the dominant and most saleable part of an individual's background. When this individual graduates, the date of graduation and any honors or high GPA information will be added to this section.

Activities: This section has been deleted—it is of minor relevance at this time.

Sample Résumé: Building Block #6
Master's Degree Individual Pursuing Next Job
(*Page 2 of Sample Résumé*)

| | **Prudential Securities**, Inc. New York, NY | summer 1999 |
| | Intern to portfolio managers | |

Education: **New York College,** New York, NY   9/04–5/06
      *Master of Business Administration

    Lafayette College, Westville, PA   2002
      *Bachelor of Arts Degree/English Major
      *Dean's List/GPA 3.5

Computer Skills: Microsoft Word, PowerPoint, Excel, Internet

REFERENCES UPON REQUEST

Résumé Comments: Building Block #7
Employed Individual Seeking a Job Change
(Chronological/Functional)

With a solid foundation for a career in media planning and buying, it is appropriate for this candidate to shift to a "chronological/functional" format. This will provide the employer with an overall combined view of the applicant's experience and responsibilities in a more expanded manner.

However, if you choose, a traditional "chronological" format can be used as well, as shown in the next example.

Format: Combined chronological/functional. Note different design that is compatible with this format versus "traditional" résumé on next page.

Name/Address: Note that the e-mail address supplied is the *personal* e-mail, not the office e-mail address. (It would be inappropriate to receive job search–related communication at an office e-mail address.)

Objective: Job objective changed to reflect experience and new goals.

Business Experience: In this example, the individual did not attend graduate school, but went directly into business. Therefore, this is the first résumé revision since graduating college.

Add company name and details for first full-time job.

Activities: This section is added back. Association membership complements business experiences.

Sample Résumé: Building Block #7
Employed Individual Seeking a Job Change
(Chronological/Functional)

Tracy Richards

900 West 8 Street
New York, NY 12345
212-555-0123/richardst@mindnet.com

Objective

To apply my previous media planning/buying experience and knowledge toward a media supervisor's position at (name of company).

Business Experience

Yates Advertising, New York, NY   9/02–Present

As senior media planner, worked closely with advertising agency account executives and Roth Pharmaceuticals' management group to determine the appropriate media strategy, and the corresponding print budget allocations for the national rollout of Sparkle mouthwash.

—Researched and analyzed the various print mediums that would most effectively and efficiently communicate with the identified target groups
—Planned and wrote the print media proposal based on a $7 million budget
—Negotiated rates and value-added packages with magazine and newspaper publishers
—Presented final media proposals to Yates Advertising account management, and subsequently to Roth Pharmaceuticals' brand group
—Currently responsible for day-to-day print activity

Other Experience

The A&E Network, New York, NY   summer 2001
Intern to creative team that produced promotional television spots

Horizon Media, New York, NY   summer 2000
Intern to Account Management Groups for:
A&E Network, History Channel, and GEICO

Prudential Securities, Inc. New York, NY   summer 1999
Intern to portfolio managers

Education/Honors
Lafayette College, Westville, PA
*Bachelor of Arts Degree/English
*Dean's List/GPA 3.5

Computer Skills
Microsoft Work, PowerPoint, Excel, and Internet

Activities
Member of New York Advertising Club

REFERENCES UPON REQUEST

Résumé Comments: Building Block #8
Employed Individual Seeking a Job Change
(Chronological)

This is the traditional "chronological" format that is an alternative to the combined "chronological/functional" format on the previous page.

Objective: Change job objective.

Qualifications: This has a *very* slight functional ingredient. For a broader description, the qualification statement from #6, with the exception of the first point that refers to Master of Business Administration, can be substituted.

Activities: This section is added back. Association membership complements business experience.

Sample Résumé: Building Block #8
Employed Individual Seeking a Job Change
(Chronological)

Tracy Richards

900 West 8 Street
New York, NY 12345
212-555-0123/richardst@mindnet.com

Objective:	To apply my previous media planning/buying experience and knowledge toward a media supervisor's position at (name of company).
Qualifications:	Full understanding of the advertising agency function, interaction with the client, and the marketing chain process toward facilitating consumer awareness and demand.

Business Experience:

Yates Advertising, New York, NY   9/02–Present
Senior Media Planner
  *Media planning/buying responsibilities for
   $7 million print budget for Sparkle
   mouthwash
  *Presented media proposals to agency and
   client management
  *Supervised assistants and media planners
  *Interacted with magazine publishers,
   negotiated rates and value-added packages

Other Experience:

The A&E Network, New York, NY   summer 2001
   Intern to creative team that produced
   promotional television spots

Horizon Media, New York, NY   summer 2000
   Intern to Account Management Groups for:
   A&E Network, History Channel, and GEICO

Prudential Securities, Inc. New York, NY   summer 1999
   Intern to portfolio managers

Education:

Lafayette College, Westville, PA   2002
   *Bachelor of Arts Degree/English Major
   *Dean's List/GPA 3.5

Computer Skills: Microsoft Word, PowerPoint, Excel, Internet

Activities: Member New York Advertising Club

REFERENCES UPON REQUEST

Résumé Comments: Building Block #9
Employed Individual Seeking a Career Change

This is where an individual has spent several years in a given field with one or more companies. After the test of time, it is concluded that it is not the right career path. A change is needed.

For appropriate reasons, the résumé again expands to two pages.

Format: For this situation, a chronological résumé with a slight functional ingredient ("qualifications") is used.

Objective: Update to reflect new career field/position desired.

Qualifications: Add experiences and skills pertinent to new pursuit. Under the heading of "you never know," this is where volunteer work can pay off again (with the relationship between tutoring and education).

Professional Experience: Add new experiences required for career change, in this case, student teaching assignments.

(continued)

Sample Résumé: Building Block #9
Employed Individual Seeking a Career Change

Tracy Richards

900 West 8 Street
New York, NY 12345
212-555-0123/richardst@mindnet.com

Objective: To apply my previous experiences in advertising, communications, and tutoring toward a career in elementary education at (name of school).

Qualifications:
*New York State Certification/kindergarten to sixth grade
 *Balanced business and student teaching credentials
 *Tutored elementary age children for six years (volunteer)
 *Excellent communication and presentation skills
 *Creative, clear, and simple delivery of subject matter
 *Organized and efficient work habits
 *Ability to allow learning to be fun
 *Effective people skills/team player

Professional Experience:

Washington Irving Elementary School, 1/05–4/05
Tarrytown, NY
Student Teacher, Fourth Grade
 *Designed and executed interdisciplinary
   thematic unit in social studies, language arts,
   and art
 *Implemented daily social studies and
   language arts lessons
 *Assisted with daily classroom activities
   and routines
 *Participated in team meetings
 *Aided students with classroom work

Bronxville Elementary School, Bronxville, NY   10/04–12/04
Field Observation, Fifth Grade
 *Assessed students' homework, classroom work, and tests
 *Led reading groups in discussion and questions
 *Constructed a language arts assignment
 *Participated in staff development and grade-level meetings

Field Observation, First Grade
 *Assisted with daily classroom activities and routines
 *Instructed small, guided reading groups
 *Assisted students with classroom work
 *Performed student assessments
 *Participated in grade-level meetings

(continued)

Sample Résumé: Building Block #9
Employed Individual Seeking a Career Change
(Page 2 of Résumé Comments)

Education: Add Master of Science in Teaching degree, graduation date, and certification number.

Honors: Add accomplishments.

Sample Résumé: Building Block #9
Employed Individual Seeking a Career Change
(*Page 2 of Sample Résumé*)

Tracy Richards

212-555-0123
richardst@mindnet.com

Other Experience:	**Yates Advertising**, New York, NY Senior Media Planner Responsibilities included: media analysis and planning, negotiating rates and value-added packages, the preparation/presentation of media proposals to Yates Advertising, and client management	9/02–6/04
	The A&E Network, New York, NY Intern to creative team that produced promotional television spots	summer 2001
	Horizon Media, New York, NY Intern to Account Management Groups for: A&E Network, History Channel, and GEICO	summer 2000
	Prudential Securities, Inc., New York, NY Intern to portfolio managers	summer 1999
Education:	**Fordham University**, Tarrytown, NY *Master of Science in Teaching *New York State Certification Provisional Certification number: 000000000 *Den's List/GPA 3.4	June 2005
	Lafayette College, Westville, PA *Bachelor of Arts Degree/English Major *Dean's List/GPA 3.5	May 2002
Honors:	**Kappa Delta Pi:** International Honors Society in Education	
Computer Skills:	Microsoft Word, PowerPoint, Excel, and Internet	

REFERENCES UPON REQUEST

Résumé Comments: Building Block #10
Previously Employed Individual Re-entering the Job Market

Functional formats are used to elaborate on an individual's experiences and credentials or to minimize attention to periods of unemployment, commonly associated with stay-at-home moms or dads re-entering the work force.

A well-composed résumé with realistic goals is important. At this time you simply want an opportunity to get a foot back in the door, and show that you can be a productive and valued employee.

Format: Functional. Note how the style goes from concise sentences to a paragraph style that allows for broad description.

Background and Experience: These sections account for the vast majority of this résumé. The point is to immediately call attention to experiences and credentials and downplay employment dates.

For that reason the dates are tucked away so that they are not easily or initially seen. The objective is to impress the reader with solid credentials first.

(continued)

Sample Résumé: Building Block #10
Previously Employed Individual Re-entering the Job Market

Tracy Richards

543 Laguna Drive
Scarsdale, CA 98765
310-555-0123/richardst@mindnet.com

Objective: To apply my advertising agency experience toward a similar position in (name of company) corporate media department.

Background: Eight years of advertising agency experience beginning as an assistant planner at Yates Advertising, Inc. and rising to Vice President/Group Media Director at DDB&O, Inc.

Heavily involved with media print planning responsibilities for the national rollout of Roth Pharmaceuticals' Sparkle mouthwash, and corresponding rate and value-added negotiations with magazine and newspaper publishers.

In addition to other senior media management responsibilities on Smyth Foods, Roth Pharmaceuticals, and Rochester Insurance, was assigned to head up the media effort for the 2004 Republican Presidential campaign. This assignment played an important role in George Bush's election, and generated contacts at various government levels.

A broad and in-depth background has provided a full understanding of the procedures and functions of the advertising agency business, and the relationship and interaction with client management, including the process and philosophy behind the facilitation of consumer awareness and demand.

Experience: **Leadership:** Responsible for a team of thirty media supervisors, media planners, and assistants. Provided direction, a teamwork mentality, motivation, and performance reviews.

Creativity: Promoted and encouraged media team to think outside the box in order to stand out from competition and gain a greater share of mind. This approach succeeded and often achieved the desired results at a lower cost.

Communications: Excellent interpersonal, writing, verbal, and listening skills. Each is essential for the understanding of an

Résumé Comments: Building Block #10
Previously Employed Individual Re-entering the Job Market
(*Page 2 of Résumé Comments*)

Education: Listing the graduation year is optional. Remember it's a roundabout way of determining one's approximate age (an illegal question to ask outright).

Dean's List and GPA are omitted; no longer relevant.

Sample Résumé: Building Block #10
Previously Employed Individual Re-entering the Job Market
(*Page 2 of Sample Résumé*)

---

assignment and/or problem and for subsequent communication and discussions. As advertising agency representatives it is imperative to be well informed, articulate, and possess savvy presentation skills.

Research Analysis: Fluent with all aspects of standard media industry research sources employed for print and broadcast audience, rating and cost efficiency comparisons, ad effectiveness, and consumer purchase patterns and preferences.

Employment:	**DDB&O, Inc.**, New York, NY	6/00–7/08
	*Vice President/Group Media Director	
	Yates Advertising, New York, NY	9/98–6/00
	*Senior Media Planner	

Education: **Lafayette College**, Westville, PA
                    *Bachelor of Arts Degree/English Major

REFERENCES UPON REQUEST

Differences Between Traditional and Scanned Résumé Formats

Traditional

A traditional format allows for a résumé to be designed and laid out with all the bells and whistles: italics, bold, underscores, bullets, symbols, horizontal and vertical lines, boxes, borders, graphics, etc. These call maximum attention to specific items and draw the reader's eye to particular points. This is contrasted by the changes that are necessary to successfully scan a résumé. Compare the two examples on the following pages and you will see a big difference—and the price you pay for speed.

Scanned

In order to be assured of successfully scanning a résumé, certain precautions should be taken. While some technology is capable of transmitting most features, not all will. Therefore, it is best to assume the worst and eliminate the amenities. Sometimes it is better to play it safe. Here are some hints:

—Use asterisks rather than bullets, which may not transmit.

—Bold font can be expressed as all-caps.

—Slashes (/) should have a space before and after the symbol (i.e., 1 / 1), so that it is easier to transmit and read. Same goes for dashes.

—Underscores won't come through, so make sure your e-mail address doesn't have any.

Sample Résumé: "Traditional" Format

Tracy Richards

900 West 8 Street
New York, NY 12345
212-555-0123/*richardst@mindnet.com*

Objective: To apply my previous experience and knowledge in advertising media and graduate school toward an assistant brand manager position at (name of company).

Qualifications:
*Advertising agency exposure to brand management at client meetings
*Understanding of interaction between advertising agency and client
*Familiarity with the relationship between marketing, media, product design, distribution, and the role that advertising plays to promote and facilitate consumer awareness and demand
*Creative, efficient, organized worker
*Promoted from assistant media planner to media planner to senior media planner within 18 months

**Business
Experience:** Yates Advertising, New York, NY   9/02–6/04
Senior Media Planner
   *Media planning/buying responsibilities for
    $7 million print budget for Sparkle
    mouthwash
   *Presented media proposals to agency
    and client
   *Supervised assistants and media planners
   *Interacted with magazine publishers,
    negotiated rates and value-added packages

**Other
Experience:** The A&E Network, New York, NY   summer 2001
   Intern to creative team that produced
   promotional television spots

Horizon Media, New York, NY   summer 2000
   Intern to Account Management Groups for:
   A&E Network, History Channel, and GEICO

Sample Résumé: "Traditional" Format
(Page 2 of Sample Résumé)

	Prudential Securities, Inc., New York, NY	summer 1999
	Intern to portfolio managers	
Education:	**New York College**, New York, NY	2006
	*Master of Business Administration	
	*President's List/GPA 3.7	
	Lafayette College, Westville, PA	2002
	*Bachelor of Arts Degree/English Major	
	*Dean's List/GPA 3.5	
Computer Skills:	Microsoft Word, PowerPoint, Excel, and Internet	

REFERENCES UPON REQUEST

Sample Résumé: "Scanned" Format

Tracy Richards

900 West 8 Street
New York, NY 10002
212 - 555 - 0123 / richardst@mindnet.com

OBJECTIVE: To apply my previous experience and knowledge in advertising media
                    and graduate school toward an assistant brand manager position at
                    (name of company).

QUALIFICATIONS: *Advertising agency exposure to brand management
                       at client meetings
                    *Understanding of interaction between advertising
                       agency and client
                    *Familiarity with the relationship between
                       marketing, media, product design, distribution,
                       and the role that advertising plays to promote
                       and facilitate consumer awareness and demand
                    *Creative, efficient, organized worker
                    *Promoted from assistant media planner to
                       media planner to senior media planner within
                       18 months

BUSINESS   YATES ADVERTISING, New York, NY   9/02 – 6/04
EXPERIENCE: Senior Media Planner
                       *Media planning / buying responsibilities for
                          $7 million print budget for Sparkle mouthwash
                       *Presented media proposals to agency and client
                       *Supervised assistants and media planners
                       *Interacted with magazine publishers,
                          negotiated rates and value-added packages

OTHER   THE A and E NETWORK, New York, NY   summer 2001
EXPERIENCE: Intern to creative team that produced
                          promotional television spots

                    HORIZON MEDIA, New York, NY   summer 2000
                       Intern to Account Management Groups for:
                       A and E Network, History Channel, and GEICO

                    PRUDENTIAL SECURITIES, INC.,   summer 1999
                    New York, NY
                       Intern to portfolio managers

Sample Résumé: "Scanned" Format
(Page 2 of Sample Résumé)

EDUCATION: NEW YORK COLLEGE, New York, NY   2006
                  *Master of Business Administration
                  *President's List / GPA 3.7

                  LAFAYETTE COLLEGE, Westville, PA   2002
                  *Bachelor of Arts Degree / English Major
                  *Dean's List / GPA 3.5

COMPUTER   Microsoft Word, PowerPoint, Excel, and Internet
SKILLS:

REFERENCES UPON REQUEST

Part 3

Sample Letters

Letter writing is extremely important under any circumstance, but even more so when searching for a job. It is the very first impression that a prospective employer will have of you. If the letter is poorly composed, too long, or visually unfriendly, that individual may be turned off and never finish reading it. Consequentially your résumé will probably not be reviewed either. Bottom line: blown effort and opportunity.

Types of Letters

Inquiry:
—Advertised position
—Direct contact with company
—Internship
—Networking lead
—Informational interview request
—Re-entering job market (after period of absence)

Follow-up:
—Thank-you to network referral person
—Thank-you to informational interview individual
—*After* scheduling interview, but *before* interview
—Initial interview thank-you
—Second follow-up letter (to initial interview)

Situational Follow-up:

—Job acceptance
—Job rejection
—Job withdrawal
—Declining job

Suggested Paragraph-by-Paragraph Contents

Remember:

—Keep the letter short
—Limit to 3–4 paragraphs (maximum)
—Approximately 12–15 sentences in total
—Single space sentences/double space paragraphs
—Use broad margins to help fill out page
—"Block" format is organized and easy to read
—12-point typeface (i.e., Arial, Times New Roman)
—20–24 lb. white/off-white stationery (only)
—Address individual by name and title
—Only Ms. or Mr.
—Check grammar/spelling
—Minimize use of the word "I"

Letter Structure

There are no set rules or order, but these guidelines may help to organize the flow and structure of the letter.

Paragraph One

—State why you are writing: personal referral, response to employment ad, college career service office lead, etc.
—Indicate position or area of business desired.

Paragraph Two

—State why you are qualified for the position.
—Describe your achievements and accomplishments relating to this area of business.

—Emphasize qualities that you have that are relevant to the job: i.e., if sales, outgoing, likeable personality, strong people and communication skills, determined, team mentality, etc.

Paragraph Three (if necessary)

—Here you may want to expand on a specific results-oriented experience or assignment.

Paragraph Four

—Thank individual for their time and consideration in advance (of scheduling interview).

—Request an interview.

—State that you will call to schedule an appointment (give specific date).

Sample Cover Letters (*with* Résumé)

Sample Cover Letter:
Initial Internship

Date
Address
City, State

Name
Address
City, State

Dear Name:

At the suggestion of the Lafayette College Career Services Director, John Doe, I am writing in pursuit of a 2005 summer internship in the Yates Advertising media department.

Based on my interest in the media business through college courses and informational interviews, Mr. Doe thought that I would be a good fit and contributor to your department's productivity, while profiting from the exposure and environment at Yates Advertising.

I hope that you will provide me with the opportunity to work for you this summer and to participate in the challenges of media planning.

Thank you in advance for your time and consideration. I look forward to the pleasure of meeting you and will call next Thursday to schedule an appointment.

Sincerely,

Tracy Richards
(phone number)
cc: John Doe

Sample Cover Letter:
Second or Third Internship

Date
Address
City, State

Name
Address
City, State

Dear Name:

At the suggestion of the Lafayette College Career Services Director, John Doe, I am writing in pursuit of a 2005 summer internship in the DDB&O, Inc. media department.

Based on my enthusiasm for the media business and previous internships with Yates Advertising and Horizon Media, Mr. Doe thought that I would be a good fit and contributor to your department's productivity, while profiting from experiencing the culture of DDB&O, Inc.

Through my exposure to the advertising business, I recognize DDB&O, Inc. as an industry leader and an advertising agency that I would like to intern with. Accordingly, I hope that you will provide me with the opportunity to work for you this summer and to participate in the challenges of media planning.

Ms. Forbes, thank you in advance for your time and consideration. I look forward to the pleasure of meeting you and will call next Tuesday to schedule an appointment.

Sincerely,

Tracy Richards
(phone number)
cc: John Doe

Sample Cover Letter:
Advertised Position

Date
Address
City, State

Name
Address
City, State

Dear Name:

This letter is in response to the elementary school teacher position that was advertised in the *Chicago Tribune* on Sunday, July 24, 2005.

My two years of experience as an assistant teacher at The Hobbs School, preceded by a master's degree in Elementary Education from Fordham University, appear to be an excellent match for the requirements set forth in your ad.

Enclosed is a copy of my résumé detailing my various responsibilities, and the corresponding qualities that I can bring to The Landmark School and its students.

Thank you in advance for your time and consideration. I look forward to the pleasure of meeting you, and will call you next Wednesday to schedule an appointment.

Sincerely,

Tracy Richards
(phone number)

Sample Cover Letter:
Direct Contact (Cold Call)

Date
Address
City, State

Name
Address
City, State

Dear Name:

During the past five years, I have developed a solid foundation in pharmaceutical sales ranging from an entry-level position to district manager. My intent is to continue this career path, and I would like to do so with Moore Pharmaceuticals.

Accordingly, I am requesting an interview for the purpose of describing my background and qualifications, and to explore possible opportunities with your company. I am certain that I can contribute to sales growth and corporate productivity given my determination, work ethic, and previous performances.

Thank you in advance for your time and consideration. I look forward to the pleasure of speaking with you, and will call next Tuesday to schedule an appointment. Meanwhile, enclosed is a copy of my résumé for your review.

Sincerely,

Tracy Richards
(phone number)

Sample Cover Letter:
Networking Lead

Date
Address
City, State

Name
Address
City, State

Dear Name:

A mutual friend, John Adams, suggested that I contact you regarding an entry-level editorial position at *People Weekly*.

During the past three summers I had editorial internships at the *St. Louis Post Dispatch,* NBC, and *Newsweek*. The latter was particularly exciting and has steered me toward a career path in magazine publishing.

As a regular reader of *People* for many years, I relate well to the editorial content and understand the market to which it is targeted. Accordingly, this May I will graduate with a Bachelor of Arts Degree in Journalism from St. Louis University, and would like to begin a career at *People Weekly.*

To that end, I would appreciate the opportunity to describe my credentials and qualifications and respectfully request an interview at your convenience. Enclosed is my résumé for your review.

Thank you in advance for your time and consideration. I look forward to the pleasure of meeting you, and will call next Thursday to schedule an appointment.

Sincerely,

Tracy Richards
(phone number)
cc: John Adams

Sample Cover Letter:
Re-entering the Work Force

Date
Address
City, State

Name
Address
City, State

Dear Name:

Following twelve years of experience in nursing and an additional three in a part-time capacity, I am prepared to re-enter the work force on a full-time basis, and would like to do so as a staff nurse at Memorial Hospital.

My previous positions as a staff, intensive care, and operating room nurse provide me with a broad and comprehensive understanding for medical procedures, patient care, and hospital organization. In today's world of an aging population and growing need for highly skilled nurses, I believe that I can complement the quality reputation that Memorial Hospital has earned.

If your schedule permits, I would like to arrange an appointment to discuss my qualifications in detail and explore possible opportunities at Memorial Hospital. Accordingly, I will contact your office next week.

Meanwhile, I look forward to the pleasure of meeting you and have enclosed a copy of my résumé for your review.

Sincerely,

Tracy Richards
(phone number)

Sample Cover Letter:
Thank-you *After* Scheduling an Initial Interview, but *Before* the Actual Interview

Date
Address
City, State

Name
Address
City, State

Dear Name:

It was a pleasure speaking with you today, and thank you for scheduling an interview with me for (date) at (time).

I am very excited to have the opportunity to discuss my background and qualifications regarding a computer programming position at (company name), and how my work ethic and determination can benefit your company.

Enclosed is a copy of my résumé for your further review.

Thank you for your time and interest.

Sincerely,

Tracy Richards
(phone number)

Sample Letters (*Without* Résumé)

Sample Letter:
Informational Interview

Date
Address
City, State

Name
Address
City, State

Dear Name:

I am writing for the purpose of requesting an informational interview with the (name of company).

Presently, I am a senior at Loyola College in Baltimore, Maryland, and am very interested in pursuing a career in commercial real estate. While I interned with John Baker Real Estate last summer, I feel that more exposure is needed before making an initial commitment to this business.

If your schedule permits, I would greatly appreciate the benefit of your knowledge and experience. Accordingly, I will call next Wednesday to schedule an appointment.

Thank you in advance for your time. I look forward to the pleasure of speaking with you.

Sincerely,

Tracy Richards
(phone number)

Sample Letter:

Thank-you *After* Scheduling an Informational Interview, but *Before* the Actual Interview

Date
Address
City, State

Name
Address
City, State

Dear Name:

It was a pleasure speaking with you today, and thank you for scheduling an informational interview with me for (date) at (time).

I am very excited to have the opportunity to meet you and to have the chance to learn about the commercial real estate industry, and the growth potential that it offers young job seekers.

In a cluttered business world it is difficult to determine the proper career to pursue. Accordingly, I thank you for taking the time to help me with this thought process.

I look forward to the pleasure of meeting you.

Sincerely,

Tracy Richards
(phone number)

Sample Letter:
Thank-you to Informational Interviewer

Date
Address
City, State

Name
Address
City, State

Dear Name:

It was a pleasure to meet you today. Thank you for being so generous with your time.

I very much appreciated your descriptions and opinions regarding the positions most appropriate to an immediate and long-range career path in civil engineering. Your insightful suggestions will be extremely helpful toward allowing me to narrow my focus in a disciplined manner.

Again, thank you. I will be sure to stay in touch and apprise you of my progress.

Sincerely,

Tracy Richards
(phone number)

Sample Letter:
Follow-up to Initial Interview

Date
Address
City, State

Name
Address
City, State

Dear Name:

It was a pleasure meeting you today, and thank you for taking the time to acquaint me with the Wachovia Bank corporate structure and the corresponding position as Assistant Director of Human Resources.

As our conversation progressed, so too did my enthusiasm and determination to secure this position. The chemistry seemed right, and my previous experiences with personnel, compensation, benefits, and training within large corporations complement your requirements.

Additionally, my work ethic and organizational, communication, and interpersonal skills are excellent and will allow me to function well in this managerial capacity. I strongly believe that I can succeed at Wachovia Bank and contribute to corporate organization.

Again, thank you for your time and consideration. I look forward to speaking with you soon and will call on Friday, as suggested.

Sincerely,

Tracy Richards
(phone number)

Sample Letter:
Second Follow-up to Initial Interview

Date
Address
City, State

Name
Address
City, State

Dear Name:

Again, thank you for your time on Monday and for the opportunity to compete for the marketing research analyst position at Fitzgerald Foods, Inc.

During our conversation, we briefly discussed new research techniques and their application to supermarket sales trends. Today's *Wall Street Journal* ran an article on that very subject, and emphasized the substantial cost saving benefits related specifically to inventory, warehousing, and shipping. It was a fascinating article and truly allowed me to appreciate the full magnitude of your comments.

Additionally, I want to reinforce my continued desire to work for Fitzgerald Foods. Beyond a solid knowledge base, I will bring a high level of enthusiasm, sound work ethic, and a teamwork approach to my job. Hopefully, you will provide me with the opportunity to achieve this goal and contribute toward the future success and growth of Fitzgerald Foods, Inc.

Thank you for your time and further consideration. I will call next week as suggested.

Sincerely,

Tracy Richards
(phone number)

Sample Letter:
Thank-you to Networking Referral Person

Date
Address
City, State

Name
Address
City, State

Dear Name:

I would like to extend my sincere thanks for referring me to Caine Financial Services.

As you indicated, Catherine Bennis was very helpful and generous with her time, and outlined various career paths that are appropriate to my interests and the corresponding qualifications for each. A next step is in place as I am scheduled to meet with the gentleman responsible for their corporate training program.

This is all very exciting and I will be certain to keep you apprised of my progress.

Again, thank you for your help.

Sincerely,

Tracy Richards
(phone number)

Sample Letter:
Follow-up to Job Acceptance
(More Formal)

Date
Address
City, State

Name
Address
City, State

Dear Name:

Thank you very much for your recent call and invitation to join O'Brasky, Prior &
Marcotullio as an elder care attorney. I appreciate your support and confidence, and
look forward to the pleasure of working together.

The terms of your offer are perfectly acceptable, specifically: $60,000 salary, bonus
based on performance, standard company-paid health and medical benefits, and a July
10 starting date. As discussed, a detailed letter of confirmation is forthcoming from
your office.

I am anxious to embrace my responsibilities and contribute to the success and growth
of this fine law firm.

Again, thank you for this opportunity and your valued guidance.

Sincerely,

Tracy Richards
(phone number)

Sample Letter:
Follow-up to Job Acceptance
(Less Formal)

Date
Address
City, State

Name
Address
City, State

Dear Name:

I would like to take this time to thank you for your invitation to join O'Brasky, Prior & Marcotullio as an elder care attorney, and for your confidence and support.

This opportunity parallels my objectives and represents an exciting moment in my career. I look forward to the challenges of this position and to contributing to the growth of (O'Brasky, Prior & Marcotullio).

Again, thank you and I look forward to seeing you on (date).

Sincerely,

Tracy Richards
(phone number)

Sample Letter:
Follow-up to Job Rejection

Date
Address
City, State

Name
Address
City, State

Dear Name:

While I am disappointed that I was not ultimately chosen for the assistant field manager's position at Newnham Resources, Inc., I do want to thank you for your time and consideration throughout the interview process.

I learned a good deal about the oil refining industry, which has served as reinforcement for my pursuit of a job in this industry.

My interest in someday working for Newnham Resources remains steadfast. Therefore, I would appreciate being considered for future opportunities, and will stay in contact and keep you apprised of my status.

Thank you and I hope that our paths will again cross.

Sincerely,

Tracy Richards
(phone number)

Sample Letter:
Job Withdrawal

Date
Address
City, State

Name
Address
City, State

Dear Name:

Thank you for your time and for considering me for the corporate accounting position at Jenney, Fuchs & Lilley, LLP.

Due to a recent decision to relocate to the West Coast, I respectfully request that my name be withdrawn from consideration.

I have a high regard for you, and Jenney, Fuchs & Lilley as a company. Accordingly, I would like to maintain contact, and will e-mail you from time to time to keep you apprised of my status.

Again, thank you for your understanding and for the opportunity to become acquainted.

Sincerely,

Tracy Richards
(phone number)

Sample Letter:
Declining a Job Offer

Date
Address
City, State

Name
Address
City, State

Dear Name:

I would like to thank you for the very flattering invitation to join the Defe Veterinary practice. However, I must respectfully decline your kind offer at this time.

A position at a major animal medical center has become available, which I have accepted. This is a unique opportunity for accelerated experience in a high-volume facility, and at this early time in my career experience must be the driving factor. Hopefully, you will understanding the reason for my decision.

I enjoyed becoming acquainted and would like to stay in touch. Accordingly, I will e-mail you from time to time and keep you apprised of my status.

Again, thank you for your time and interest.

Sincerely,

Tracy Richards
(phone number)

Part 4

Interview Questions and Answers

Once the importance of a well-written résumé and cover letter, one's personal appearance, and etiquette are understood, the focus of the interview becomes how questions are asked and answered. After all, in the end, that is what interviewing is about. It is how the interviewer gets a feel for your substance and personality.

Types of Interview Questions

There are many types of questions that can be asked. In the spirit of conciseness and clarity, which are primary objectives of this book, three groupings have been established for your convenience.

Standard/Traditional Questions: These questions will probe into your background, reasons for pursuing a particular industry or company, goals, skills, etc.

Behavioral Questions: Intended to obtain insight into how you think and may react in a particular environment, with a specific problem, and with fellow employees and/or clients.

Logic Questions: Designed to explore your thought process to see how you arrive at a given conclusion or answer. In most cases, the interviewer is not interested in the exact answer, but more concerned with how you think through the problem.

Always assume that a good portion of questioning will be of the standard/traditional variety. The second most popular will be behavioral, while logic questions may be more appropriate for problem solving jobs, such as engineering, consultants, and the like. Knowledge of why these different types of questions are asked, and what their intents are, can be of obvious help insofar as structuring your responses.

This section provides sample questions and answers that will point you in the right direction and help get you started.

Questions are limited only by an interviewer's curiosity and imagination. Therefore, it is not possible to provide a list of all conceivable questions that can be asked. However, some of the most commonly asked standard/traditional and behavioral questions are provided. Logic questions are abstract and inventive and not predictable. In this case, examples are given based on style and hypothetical content.

Remember: Try to craft your responses so that they relate back to a benefit (in terms of business) for the prospective employer, particularly for standard/traditional and behavioral questions.

Standard/Traditional Questions and Answers

Q. *Tell me about yourself.*

A. This is usually asked at the outset of an interview and used as a jumping-off point that leads to other questions and probing.

This is where you should be able to summarize your background in sixty to ninety seconds, as previously discussed.

Start with: where you were raised, where you attended college, any internships you had, accomplishments or achievements, and what you want to do professionally.

Q. *Why do you want to work in this business (or industry)?*

A. Here you must be ready with a very concrete reason for this decision.

Most logically this will tie back to a personal experience, a job, internship, or being influenced by a course of study, a professor, or mentor. It should *never* be merely a random choice.

Q. *Why do you want to work for this company?*

A. Again, a very specific answer should be prepared and ready. Example: "Through previous job experiences or internships, I became aware of this company and recognized it as an industry leader. Further research revealed a practice for thorough training and development, and a policy of promoting from within. Both served to reinforce my decision."

Q. *What do you think are important trends in this business?*

A. This answer is a result of the research you did. Is it an emerging industry on the cutting edge? Fast-changing technology? And so on.

Q.   What do you know about our company, problems, trends?

A.   Know the company's position in the industry (leader, number two, etc.). Are they burdened with rapidly increasing costs? Product demand? Projected growth for the next three to five years?

Q.   What are your goals and expectations?

A.   Example: "I want to work for company XYZ because of its leadership position in the industry, and its reputation for producing quality products and services. I expect to receive on-going performance critique and direction so that I stay on a continuous learning curve, make a maximum contribution to the company, and expand my responsibilities."

Q.   Where do you expect to be in one, three, or five years?

A.   Here specific job titles and responsibilities are not expected, but rather an indication of your thinking. Example: "As someone new to the business, I will likely be in a learning mode for the first year or so. As I demonstrate my ability to perform effectively, I would expect to have expanded responsibilities with the gradual development of a solid foundation. At this juncture, I hope that my knowledge of the job (business) and contributions to the organization will be fully recognized and rewarded."

Q.   What are your strengths and weaknesses?

A.   This is one you really want to be prepared for. The strengths are easy, you know what they are: well-organized, clear thinker, analytical, self-starter, computer skills, etc. Weaknesses are tough (since we all think that we're perfect!). Be ready with one or two, but be sure they are not damaging. For example, nothing to do with tardiness, an inability to function in the mornings, leaving assignments until the last minute, etc., but something that suggests initiative, such as: "Sometimes in my eagerness, I bite off more than I should and end up in a crunch. I'm learning to monitor the load that I take on more effectively."

Q.   What skills do you have to offer?

A.   This is a fairly open-ended question since it can range from technical skills (such as computer expertise) to linguistics to interpersonal skills. Do a thorough appraisal of yourself; you may have more to offer than you think!

Q. *What accomplishments are you most proud of?*
A. Here is a wonderful opportunity to present the interviewer with insights of yourself by briefly describing several accomplishments. Maybe use one related to business or an internship where you were particularly successful with an assignment or problem and its results. A second could be social or humanitarian in nature—perhaps mentoring an underprivileged student who, because of your efforts, succeeded. A third could be leadership oriented. Leading a team to victory, serving as class president, etc. Choose examples that paint a well-rounded picture of who you are.

Q. *Will you relocate?*
A. This is a personal choice. If you say no, it may eliminate you from consideration; if you give a definitive yes, you are committed. If you are uncertain, assume the middle ground by responding with: "That is an opportunity I am willing to consider." This question may only be asked to test your flexibility, and an actual move may never materialize. If it does, you can always turn it down later. Keep your options open.

Q. *What was the last book you read (or a movie you saw)?*
A. This question is asked to get a sense of your interests. Is it a frivolous romance or spy novel or something of substance: history, investing, life-altering how-to books, etc. It's okay to mention one from both groups, as long as at least one serious book is included. Ditto for movies. (If you haven't read a good book or seen a movie lately, here's a great reason to do so!) Show that you are well-rounded and curious.

Q. *Tell me about a job or experience you liked the most.*
A. Here something that was stimulating, exciting, or gratifying in a way that is relevant to business should be stated. This might be a meaningful job or internship that opened up a new world for you or a personal involvement that relates to teamwork.

Q. *Why do you think that you are qualified for this position?*

A. Tie this response to a previous job, internship, or work that had personal value. Show that you are committed to this business, have thoroughly researched the pros and cons, have the academic credentials, a high work ethic, are determined, organized, and a self starter, have solid interpersonal skills and team player mentality. Work these types of points into the job qualifications and you will have done well.

Q. *Why do you want to change jobs?*

A. Do not be negative in a way that "bad-mouths" your current employer. If you do, the interviewer can assume that similar negativity will repeat itself in the future. Rather, be truthful, citing things like lack of advancement or challenge, a desire to work for a larger (or smaller) company, to work for the industry leader, and so on. Be sure the reasons are concrete.

Q. *What salary do you seek?*

A. If you are uncertain what the job pays, a good response is: "My primary objective is to work for the XYZ Company. While money is important it is a secondary consideration—I am sure I will be treated fairly." If you were able to research the salary range you can begin by saying: "I understand that the industry is paying $00,000–$00,000 for this type of position. However, my primary objective is to work for the XYZ Company," and I am sure that I will be treated fairly.

This provides an answer to the question, while also demonstrating where your first priority lies—in working for that company. Do not let money appear to be a deal breaker. If their offer is truly unacceptable, you can always turn it down then.

Q. *Describe how your career direction has changed.*

A. Provide a concrete answer based on experience. Example: "College internships in marketing encouraged me to follow that direction after graduation. After working as an assistant marketing analyst for a year, it became apparent that my outgoing personality and energy level were more suited for sales. My management agreed, and gave me that opportunity several months later."

Q. *What are your greatest assets?*

A. This is an easy one—the following should cover the bases: "The most important possession an individual can have is his or her reputation. Putting forth a truthful approach to life, a solid work ethic, quality performance, reliability, and an unselfish team-oriented mentality will get you far in life."

Q. *How do you handle short deadlines?*

A. Organizational skills are the key to managing deadlines. Keep planning as simple and uncomplicated as possible. Establish a schedule (a timeline) and a corresponding to-do list—then adhered to them. Doing so gives you a level of control.

Delegate and tackle each element individually, and bring them together at the end. Otherwise chaos will rule.

Q. *How do you combine traditional business practices with creativity?*

A. At the root of every success is a solid business plan. A clear strategy complements a creative approach to achieving a goal. Traditional business practices and a unique execution can be effective partners.

Q. *How would your friends describe you?*

A. Be careful with this one—this is another way of saying, "How would you describe yourself?" Do not be too flowery on the one hand, or overly modest on the other. Set forth a truthful assessment of your personality and qualities. Be believable.

Q. *Describe a situation where you failed.*

A. This should not be a damaging example, but perhaps one that ties back to an internship or early job. In this way inexperience can be the culprit.

Several examples may be: not being properly prepared, not allowing enough time, not double-checking or proofing work, etc.

Q. *How will your previous experiences contribute to business success?*

A. Whatever your answer is, a good connection is teamwork—the core of business success. Earlier in the book we discussed how being a member of a sports team served as a wonderful model. You could say something like, "Relying on teammates to collectively achieve victory is the best way to win. I experienced this firsthand in sports, and understand its importance and value in business."

Q. *How do you feel about working late hours or on weekends?*

A. This is obvious. You must have the proper attitude and understanding for what it takes to get the job done. If it's putting in extra hours, so be it. In the end you will be part of the team that delivered the goods. Be willing and eager—it will pay dividends sooner or later.

Behavioral Questions and Answers

Q. *Are you the type of person who loves to win or hates to lose? Why?*

A. This is my very favorite question because of the passion and determination that can be implied. Everyone likes to win. It is human nature. It is also fun, whether it is a prize, a competition, or landing a job. But not everyone has the same constitution. While winning is the ideal, losing may be an accepted reality (for most). For others, with deeper passion and determination, losing is not an option. They clearly *hate* to lose. Perhaps this becomes the more powerful answer?

There is a fine line here, and the structure and tone of the response can have an impact one way or another. Therefore, when replying to this type of question, it is important to articulate your reasoning— because, depending on how the response is structured, this question can be argued both ways.

Q. *Do you prefer to work independently or with a group? Why?*

A. During the course of this book the importance of teamwork, and one's ability to work together, have been emphasized a number of times.

While parts of a project require individual work and preparation, all of the parts must join at a certain point. This is where the elements of teamwork come together for the good of a common goal. An explanation that includes both elements will illustrate your understanding and appreciation for the cornerstone of business success: teamwork.

Q.   Describe a difficult situation and how you handled it.

A.   A question of this nature will indicate your temperament, common sense, tact, and judgment in dealing with a people-related problem.

Describe the circumstance and explain the steps that you took to solve the problem (and reasons for taking them).

Q.   How do you respond to criticism?

A.   This question can give interviewers an idea for your willingness to learn, accept suggestions, and profit from the results. This is important (for them) because it ultimately impacts upon the department's performance, productivity, overall interaction, and teamwork; and whether or not the person hired will become a "project." As time consuming as business has become, someone who is stubborn or unwilling to accept criticism will generally not succeed and usually is not welcome.

Give an example of how you respond to criticism, maybe by setting your meeting to go over the problems and discovering that everyone was on the same page after all.

Q.   How do you handle defeat? Rejection?

A.   These types of questions are similar. They are meant to uncover a sense of bitterness, anger, hostility, short-temperedness, etc. A calm response with a positive spin should work here. Example: "Throughout the years, I had the opportunity to play many sports, mostly organized competition in high school and college. My parents and coaches all stressed good sportsmanship whether on the winning or losing end. As an application of those lessons, being gracious regardless of the circumstances cannot hurt, and certainly can help. The most important thing we have to offer is our reputation and the image that people have of us."

Q.   Are you aggressive or conservative?

A.   This is a test of courage and judgment. Are you a wild person or well balanced? There is an expression: "no risk, no gain." The risk should not be a long shot with little chance for success, but should be well researched to reflect up-side rewards and down-side consequences. If the reasoning and logic make sense, then the risk is minimized and worthwhile.

So, a good answer is: "I am aggressive and take risks appropriately, however I'm conservative with the basic functions and practices."

Q. *Are you comfortable working without supervision?*
A. Superiors do not want to baby-sit subordinates. Individuals who take direction well and run with it are well thought of and valued.

A response indicating the above coupled with a self-starter comment is on target. Also, allow the interviewer the comfort level of knowing that you are secure enough to ask questions if you are uncertain about particular details.

Q. *What are your feelings about working for a younger person or a female (if you are male)?*
A. There should be no hesitation in your response. If the company thinks enough of an individual, regardless of age or sex, to place them in that position, that is all that counts. Promotions and appointments should be merit related and earned. Period. Your response should express similar insight and sensitivity. It should not matter as long as the superior is qualified, fair, and helpful.

Q. *How will you complement this company/department?*
A. This is a fairly open-ended question that allows a candidate to lay out the qualities that employers are obviously looking for and impressed by. Mainly, a strong work ethic, teamwork mentality, pride in a job well done, eagerness to learn and contribute to overall success, etc. Be gracious and sincere without going overboard. Be believable.

Q. *Tell me about your time management approach to a typical workday.*
A. This really comes down to priority considerations. The things that must be acted on first, the balance second. The items that require the input, assistance, or response to or from others during the

workday when everyone is available, versus independent tasks that can be done at your discretion and leisure.

Simply framing a response to this effect will provide the interviewer with an appreciation of your understanding.

Q. *What do you do in your spare time?*

A. This question provides another opportunity for insight into your values and interests. Be balanced with this response to include strong family involvement and values that will reflect upon how you will interact with your "extended" family—your co-workers. Additionally, any volunteer work, sports, or other activities that present you as a well-rounded, caring person should be included in your response.

Q. *How do you relax?*

A. Everyone needs an outlet. Without one we cannot function properly, just as if you let a pot of water boil too long the pressure from the heat will blow the cover off. The same is true for us as human beings. We simply cannot continue to perform under stress and pressure without something giving. How we release pressure is key to job performance—and a seemingly meaningless question. But it is an important one. Some companies think so highly of relaxation and stress reduction that they provide on-site fitness centers, health club memberships, and yoga classes to employees. You should also mention one or two stress-relieving activities that are non-physical in nature, like crossword puzzles, music, massage, manicures, etc. This shows that you have more than one method of dealing with stress.

Q. *How do your outside activities contribute to a business teamwork mentality?*

A. Early on in the book, interviewing was described as a competition where the winner takes all. Similarly, business is a competition with one company or team going head-to-head with others. The team that is generally most successful is the one with good camaraderie, unselfishness, and an understanding and willingness to function as a group.

The analogy of a musical chorus comes to mind. One voice alone has little impact of depth, but a group of forty to fifty people singing in harmony with each other becomes strong and powerful. Your response should reflect this value and understanding.

Q. *Describe a problem that you had with a co-worker.*

A. This is a test of patience, tact, and maturity. Example: "There was a fellow salesperson who viewed several of his peers as a threat. Not the younger staff members, but the senior group. At every opportunity this person was quick to criticize, bad-mouth, or undermine the actions of the others (me included) behind their backs, while pretending to be friendly to their faces. I, as well as the others, stayed composed, confident that sooner or later this person would self-destruct. Even though it took longer than we would have liked, the person was ultimately recognized for what he was and terminated. This individual was a negative influence and certainly did not have a teamwork mindset."

Q. *How would you define personal success?*

A. Again, this is an opportunity to demonstrate your well-rounded qualities. Go beyond monetary goals and aspirations and discuss personal values. Being happy and self-fulfilled is very important. We all have to work for a long time, so we should do something that we enjoy. That's why schoolteachers and social workers, for example, dedicate themselves to relatively low-paying fields. The satisfaction they receive is payment of another kind.

This reply shows maturity and speaks volumes for determination and caring.

Q. *If you are hired, how long will you stay?*

A. In many cases the candidate will repeat the obvious answer, and one that the interviewer has heard time and again, something along the lines of: "This is a fine company, where I want to build my career and retire from."

The more appropriate and effective answer is the honest one—and the one we all know to be real: "Change is not necessary unless there is a reason. I will stay for as long as I continue to learn and be challenged, and progress along a steady career path."

This is a very reasonable answer, and probably not unlike the personal feeling of the interviewer. Who in their right mind would stay unhappily in a dead-end job? Any other response is not believable.

Q.   *How do you prefer to communicate?*

A.   Here you should cover all of your bases to establish equal capabilities, but show a preference and state why. Example: "I feel comfortable with my overall communication skills, but always feel that verbal face-to-face situations work well for me. Not only do I feel that my personality and level of confidence complements this style, but it also allows for the added opportunity to respond or interject points that grow out of the conversation. Written communication does not permit that flexibility."

Responding in this way allows the interviewer to see that you are looking for that competitive edge—a subject that has been emphasized throughout this book.

Q.   *How do you prepare for deadline assignments?*

A.   Again, this is a function of organizational skills and priorities. Creating a timeline for assignments and a priority list is key to this success. Being disorganized and uncertain is the kiss of death! Additionally, knowing the work habits and dependability of those who you have involved in your project is very important.

Where possible build in a cushion, because "Murphy's Law" is almost certain to raise its ugly head: "What can go wrong, will."

Saying you do all these things will show good planning and awareness—and showcase your level of experience.

Q.   *How do you handle unpopular decisions?*

A.   In a word: honestly—and yes, in a straightforward manner. Do not hedge, make excuses, or disguise the real facts. It is generally transparent, and the truth will come out in the end anyway. Your credibility will be tarnished, and nothing will be gained.

If it is a decision that affects you directly, there is generally nothing you can do to reverse it. So, be a good soldier. Take one for the team. It will usually profit you in one way or another in the long run although it is sometimes difficult to realize that at the moment.

Logic Questions and Answers

Q. *For what purposes would you use a brick?*

A. This is another one of my favorites. On the surface it appears to be an innocent, no-strings-attached question. But in fact it is very revealing. Note that the sentence is structured to say: For what purpose *would*—as opposed to *could*—you use a brick? Saying "*would*" implies a specific action on your part, not a suggestive thought.

Some common answers are: as a doorstopper, a weight, part of a house, a walkway, and so on. All are functional but passive uses that may reflect the personality of the interviewee; nothing aggressive or exciting that would breathe new life into a project or company.

In contrast, the response, "To throw through a window" possibly indicates a proactive risk taker, who knows that being caught will lead to consequences. However, he or she is still willing to take that chance and profit from that action. There are no innocent questions. So much can be told by so little!

Q. *You are a New York consultant and receive two assignments on the same day. One is from a British company, the other is from a company located in California. Both have the same deadline of one week. All things being equal, which assignment should be completed first?*

A. This is a relatively simple question that is intended to see how quickly you respond. Here the answer is in the time difference. England is five hours ahead of New York, California three hours behind—a swing factor of eight hours. The British company's project should be scheduled for completion first since an additional eight hours is built into the California project.

Q. Why can a good product fail?

A. Any number of answers could be given for this question. The interviewee should try to build a storyline that demonstrates his or her ability to think a problem through. Any good product can die a slow death on a store shelf if not marketed and promoted properly. Go back to some of the points that were discussed earlier in the book ("Interviewing Logic and Rationale") for a moment. These tips were related to how to market, advertise, and sell one's self when interviewing for a job. Remember, this approach was applied from product marketing, so let's return to its original intent.

—*Establish awareness: Is the product visible?* Is there sufficient advertising and promotional exposure to make consumers aware that the product exists? Are there "cents off" coupons to encourage a trial purchase? Is there adequate distribution and shelf space to allow for in-store product visibility? And so on.

—*Are product benefits clearly stated?* Consumers need a reason to switch from one product to another.

—*Have the above points created curiosity?* If not, the product will have low visibility and interest level, and is probably doomed to fail, or at best have marginal success. Also, pricing may be a factor. Is it low, high, or competitively positioned? If it is too low it may be suspect. If higher than other brands, there had better be a solid reason why.

Structuring a logical sequential response shows that you are an organized thinker. Clarity and simplicity are highly valued skills to employers.

Q. How many television sets are there in the United States?

A. This is a slightly different question to test your ability to think through a problem and arrive at an answer.

The interviewer is not interested in whether or not the answer is exact, but rather your reasoning and the step-by-step approach that you take.

So, hypothetically, let's assume that there are 97 million households in the United States, with an average of 2.4 television sets per household. By multiplying the two, you estimate a total of 232.8 million sets.

Q. *A plane departs from Los Angeles to New York City at 11:00 A.M.; another plane departs from New York City to Los Angeles at 3:30 P.M. Each is traveling at 500 mph. Which plane will be closer to Chicago when they cross? To what extent will head or tail winds be a factor?*

A. This question has a number of points that are designed as smokescreens and are intended to complicate the thought process. It is a good question to measure the interviewee's ability to cut through the unnecessary details and zero in on the essential points.

In this case, the speed and departure times have no influence on the question whatsoever. They are pure distraction. Regardless of any extra factors both planes will be equally close to Chicago when they cross (since they're at the same point). Concentrating on the "fine print" is the key.

Q. *Why is a manhole cover round?*

A. This is one of the oldest and most frequently asked logic questions. So, let's briefly answer the question. Because it is round it can be rolled; also, if it were square it could be turned and fall through the hole: a round manhole cover can't fall through.

That's it! Simple logic and visual thinking.

Q. *You have a chair with one leg shorter than the other. Do you repair one leg or shorten the other three?*

A. Ahh, once again logic and visualization come into play. It may be easier and less time-consuming to shorten the three legs, but then the chair may be too low for the table, if it is used with a table. Otherwise, it may be okay a little lower. So, there are really two correct answers to this question, depending on the situation and your point of view.

As you have probably surmised at this point, standard/traditional and behavioral questions are easier to prepare for than logic questions because they are more straightforward.

Logic questions are unpredictable and abstract without pat or rehearsed answers that can be immediately reeled off in response. So, beyond the types of logic questions that we just discussed, it is not practical to provide more examples. These cover the points and make you aware of the style that can be expected. Be prepared to think on your feet!

Questions to Ask the Interviewer

For obvious reasons, interviewers are looking to hire individuals who are intelligent, curious, and sharp. The importance of integrating thoughtful questions into your interview strategy is key to the quality image that you will project.

The following is a range of questions that you may consider asking. In addition to doing so during the interview, always be prepared with several questions in response to the interviewer's "Do you have any questions?" that is almost certain to be asked at the end of an interview.

—What is the company's philosophy (mission statement)?
—What is the corporate culture?
—How are new employees familiarized within the company?
—Is there a formal training program?
—How are employees evaluated? How often?
—Given a good performance review, how can I expect to progress within the company?
—How does someone succeed here?
—Does the company offer extended educational opportunities?
—What are the company's short- and long-term goals?
—Has the company's size increased or decreased within the past year or two? Why?
—Where can this position lead?
—As an international company, are there opportunities to work abroad?
—What do you seek in a prospective employee?
—What background or skills are most important for this position?
—Internally, which department is considered the focal point of the company? Why?

—Do the departments function individually or in concert with each other?

—What are the company's plans for growth?

—What is the key function of this job?

—How long has this position been vacant?

—As an insider, how do you see your company as being different from the competition?

—Have current employees interviewed for this job?

—Now that you have reviewed my résumé and we have spoken, do you feel that I am qualified? If so, will you recommend me for a next interview?

—Do you feel that I will fit in with your company?

—What attracted you to this company? Or, why did you come to work for this company?

—What do you enjoy most about this company?

—What is it like living in this city?

—When will you be making a hiring decision?

—What is the next step?

Save questions about salary, benefits, vacation, etc., until after you are offered the job; you will have ample opportunity at that time. Otherwise you risk sending the wrong message.

Questions That Are Illegal
for an Interviewer to Ask

While certain questions are illegal for interviewers to ask, they are sometimes asked anyway. It can be done unintentionally and out of ignorance, or intentionally. The question may be cleverly disguised to elicit the desired response without arousing suspicion or being offensive. For example, "Do you have children?" may be asked indirectly: "This position may require late hours, some weekends, and travel; how will this conflict with raising children and your family life?"

Your response must be measured and tactful, and yes, prepared. It should not connote anger or sarcasm and should not be insulting or arrogant. Remember this person controls your immediate future with this company, and will determine if you progress further with the interview process.

In this situation you have three choices; two good, one not so good. If the question is not "harmful," simply answer it. Or, respond tactfully to the tone of: "My previous positions and responsibilities were also demanding in a similar way, and did not conflict with my personal life. There should not be any concern about my ability to handle this job properly." You addressed the "concern." Referring to your "personal life" versus "family life" is specific, yet ambiguous. Two can play the same game.

You could also answer with something like, "That is a question that I am not required to answer (or do not feel comfortable answering)." With other good choices, this will only be an irritant. Why risk turning the interviewer off?

The following are examples of illegal questions that you may encounter and should be prepared to respond to.

—What is your age?

—When did you graduate college?

—What is your marital status?

—Do you live alone?

—Do you live with your parents?

—Do you have children?

—If yes, who cares for them during the day?

—What is your spouse's occupation?

—How many dependents do you have?

—What is your maiden name?

—Will late hours, weekend assignments, and/or travel interfere with raising your children and your family life?

—Are you gay or straight?

—What is your nationality?

—Where is your family from?

—What is your religion?

—Do you have any physical problems?

—Do you have any health problems?

—Do you have AIDS or HIV?

—How many sick days did you take last year?

—Were you ever arrested?

—Do you have any outside income?

Part 5:

Targeting the Right Employer

The simple effort of conducting research with a questionnaire will almost certainly separate you from the pack and provide a competitive advantage. The majority of job candidates will not think or bother to take this step. Correlate the responses, establish percentages, and report the results on a summary page. This research can be used during an interview or as part of your follow-up. Either way it can only be an impressive effort and a demonstration of how much you want this position, and the effort you will bring to your job.

Sample Employer Survey

Background

A leading manufacturer of kitchen and household products has recently introduced new packaging for their clear wrap product. The feature is a new cutting device that replaces the traditional serrated (cutting) edge found on wax paper, tin foil, and clear wraps.

The purpose of this survey is to measure consumer satisfaction and obtain pro and con comments.

The survey can be conducted among either random shoppers or by approaching shoppers who actually remove a clear wrap product from store shelves. Either way, conduct the survey inside the store. If you wait until shoppers exit the store, they are likely to be in more of a hurry and less inclined to speak with you.

Finally, limit questions and keep them brief. People are busy and will become impatient. State up front that you'll only take a minute of their time, so they know what to expect.

See sample questionnaire on the following page.

Consumer Questionnaire

---

1. Do you use a clear wrap product?

   If yes, which one?_____
      (Skip if you are surveying shoppers who actually remove a clear wrap product from the store shelf.)

   If no, terminate interview.

2. Are you a regular user of this product?_____

3. Have you ever used brand Y (your product of interest)?_____
      (Ask only if they use competitive brand)

   If so, why did you switch?_____

4. What do you like most about the product you are currently using?

   _____

5. (If the cutting edge has not been mentioned, probe.)
      Are you familiar with brand Y's new cutting device?_____

6. If yes, do you find it more effective and convenient than traditional serrated edges?_____

7. What are the primary advantages and disadvantages?

   Advantages: _____
   _____

   Disadvantages: _____
   _____

8. If not mentioned, ask if box is convenient to store in a drawer or cabinet. This is important because the cutting edge is removed from the box by the consumer, and affixed to the outside of the box. This does not allow one box to be stored flush against another.

9. Will you try this product or continue to use it?_____

Businesses and Positions Within Specific Industry Categories

The following is a list of general industries and some of the businesses and positions that are related to those fields.

The purpose is to provide an individual with options that allow him or her to remain in a given area of business without changing industries, while providing the opportunity to return to that earlier business at some future time.

Besides this benefit, it also allows an individual to continue on a given career path without sacrificing momentum, growth experience, and compensation pace.

These options can also be valuable to college students who are seeking internships within a given industry, but cannot land a position in the business of their first choice. A related business can get them in the game with valuable exposure, and allow them to trade on that experience in the future.

Accounting

—Accountant
  –Small firm specializing in maintaining day-to-day practices and income tax preparation
  –Individual company
  –Income tax specialist
—Accounting department member
  –Accounts payable/receivable
  –Operating expenses, travel, and entertainment, etc.
—Tax auditor
—Budget forecaster and planner

—Collection agent
—Payroll clerk

Advertising/Public Relations

—Copywriter
—Art director
—Commercial director/producer
—Media planning/buying
—Marketing representative
—Market researcher
—Account executive

Aeronautical

—Pilot
—Traffic controller
—Computer operator/programmer
—Maintenance worker
—Airline company employee

Architecture

—Commercial
—Residential
—Landscaping
—Interior
—Draftsman
—Review board member
—Surveyor
—Contractor

Broadcast (Radio/Television/Internet)

—Producer
—Director
—Writer

—Reporter
—Announcer
—Fashion consultant
—Researcher

Computers

—Programmer
—Technician
—Hardware engineer
—Software engineer
—Network operator
—Systems analyist

Construction

—Contractor
—Architect
—Material supply company representative
—Electrician
—Plumber
—Realtor
—Related material manufacturer
—Salesperson

Criminology

—Forensics specialist
—Investigative agent
—Law enforcement member
—Lawyer

Design

—Fashion
—Automotive
—Interior

—Exterior
—Landscaping
—Graphic

Education

—Teacher
—Teacher aide
—Coach
—Special education teacher
—Psychologist
—Tutor
—Day care provider
—Librarian
—Computer technology instructor
—Translator
—Nutritionist

Engineering

—Aerospace: Electrical, industrial, and mechanical
—Chemical: Engineering and construction, petrochemical, refineries
—Civil: Architectural, environmental, highway design, municipal, surveying
—Electrical: Aerospace/defense, automobile, automation, biomedical, communication/telecom, computer and high-tech hardware and software
—Industrial: Aerospace/defense, automotive, manufacturing
—Mechanical: Aerospace/defense, agriculture, automation, automotive, biomedical, ceramic, construction
—Nuclear: Aerospace/defense, healthcare/medicine, utility companies
—Petroleum engineer: Oil/gas exploration and production companies

Event Planning

—Corporation event planner
—Sales meeting/convention specialist
—Entertainment company planner

Financial

—Investment broker (stocks, bonds, etc.)
—Securities specialist
—Analyst
—Broadcaster
—Reporter
—Writer
—Banker (loans, mortgages, securities, insurance)
—Mortgage lender
—Financial planner
—Collection agent
—Tax accountant
—Credit card company representative
—Economist

Government

—Investigation agent
—Secret service agent
—Congressional aide
—Page

Health/Medical

—Medical doctor
—Dentist
—Chiropractor
—Physical therapist
—Dietician
—Nutritionist
—Health club employee
—Hospital worker
—Medical lab technician
—Radiologist
—Nurse care agency employee
—Pharmacist

—Veterinarian
—Nursing home company employee

Human Resources

—Corporate human resources department employee
—Executive recruiter
—Personnel agency employee

Legal

All companies, small, medium, and large, require legal assistance. Choosing a field of personal interest is a good way to narrow the selection process (i.e., sports, finance, entertainment, etc.).

Marketing

—Consultant
—Telemarketer
—Broadcasting marketer
—Writer
—Demographer
—Sales promoter
—Public relations employee
—Corporate marketing department (any industry)
—Publishing company
—Advertising agency
—Opinion poll
—Broadcast, magazine, newspaper, Internet companies
—Independent firms

Media

—Art director
—Copy director

—Television, commercial, or movie producer
—Set designer
—Music producer
—Fashion designer
—Actor
—Sound engineer
—Lighting specialist
—Sale promotional company employee
—Advertising agency
—Public relations department
—Corporate in-house department
—Independent media buying services
—Media research company
—Media tracking service

Photography

—Portrait
—Commercial
—Newspaper
—Broadcast/news
—Magazine
—Fashion
—Action

Physical Therapy

—Sports club
—Physical therapy facility
—Hospital
—Rehabilitation center
—Schools/colleges
—Sports teams
—Independent practice

Public Service

—Law enforcement official
—Public defender
—Firefighter
—Transit system employee
—Port authority employee

Publishing (Books/Magazines/Newspapers/Internet)

—Editor
—Writer
—Proofreader
—Columnist
—Reporter
—Publicist

Retail

—Buyer
—Sales promoter
—Interior designer
—Salesperson
—Model

Sales

Business is about sales; most corporations depend heavily on sales force production. Choosing a field of personal interest is important to maintain motivation and interest. This is critical because salespeople must be able to handle rejection and rebound without losing momentum.

Science

—Pharmacist
—Chemist

—Physicist
—Farmer
—Space program employee
—Geologist
—Marine biologist
—Environmentalist

Service

—Restaurant employee
—Food service employee
—Catering staff member
—Hotel employee

Social Services

—Social worker
—Local/state government agent

Sports

—Broadcaster
—Reporter
—Statistician
—Writer
—Technical (i.e., camera person)
—Producer
—Photographer
—Player
—Trainer
—Physical therapist
—Announcer
—Official/referee
—Travel coordinator
—Lawyer
—Commissioner's office employee

Technology

—Computer company
—Communications
—Manufacturing
—Airline company

Transportation

—Airlines
—Railroads
—Shipping
—Automotive
—Trucking
—Bus lines
—Public transit
—Port authority
—Car rental

You should now feel confident in your ability to interview well . . . you now have a competitive edge. So:

The stage is set. . . .

You know your cues. . . .

Now deliver your lines with the self-assurance of a business professional.

Good luck, and as they say in show business: Break a leg!

Acknowledgments

Over the course of the years, many people and experiences combine to represent an individual's career—sort of like the pieces of a puzzle that come together to create a complete picture.

The following are a few of the "puzzle pieces" that were very special in the development and progress of my life and career, individuals who unknowingly contributed to the contents of this book through the guidance and knowledge that they shared throughout the years.

Ted Kidd, my first manager and the person who taught me so much more than the basics of selling advertising space for (the original) *Life* magazine. He was firm yet fair and taught me the importance of being professional and well prepared.

Art Karlan, who made my days at *Newsweek* a total joy. His sense of humor demonstrated that business could be fun. Thanks for the lessons and memories.

People magazine is where I spent the bulk of my career and where I had the privilege of working with an extremely professional and marketing-driven management—my special thanks to Ann Moore, Nora McAniff, Peter Bauer, Paul Caine, Frank Roth, and Lou Cona for their support and input, and for the experiences that have helped in the development of this book.

My deepest thanks to my friend Betsy Hulseborsh for her encouragement and suggestions when this concept was in its infancy. Her direction was invaluable.

My biggest champion and the person to whom I am most grateful is Matt Baldacci, director of marketing at St. Martin's Press. Matt recognized the need for addressing the inadequate interviewing skills among (mostly) graduating college seniors and young professionals. His vision to fill this void and propose the publishing of this book represents an opportunity to help job seekers succeed. I thank him for his support and confidence. And to Judy—you know who you are.

To my editor, Ethan Friedman, thank you for guiding me through the editing process and offering suggestions that have improved the contents and flow of *Don't Blow the Interview*. You are a talented and gifted person.

I'd also like to thank Maura Fadden Rosenthal for the wonderful cover design and Christina MacDonald for her careful and incisive copyediting. This book is much improved through your efforts.

Good friends are to be treasured, and Andy Steigmeier is a good friend. Thank you for the time that you spent on the creative development of the *Don't Blow the Interview* workshop presentation. Without your help this project would not have gotten to its next level. Also, my appreciation to Dick Weiss, managing partner at Richard Wayne & Roberts executive recruiters for his help in providing editorial input.

To my daughter, Katie, for the many hours that she spent at her computer during the early stages of the book's development. Thank you for being so helpful and generous with your time.

Finally, how do you express your thanks when there aren't words worthy of that appreciation? My very special wife, Cathy, who worked side by side with me for the months that it took to complete this book. Her computer expertise, patience, and ability to critique and edit the manuscript were truly gifts—without which my job would have been considerably more difficult and not nearly as pleasant.

About the Author

Ralph Ferrone's forty-year career was concentrated in magazine advertising sales with Time Inc, a division of Time Warner; *People* and *Life* magazines; and *Newsweek, New York* magazine, and Norman Craig & Kummel and Doyle Dane Bernbach advertising agencies.

He is the president of Interview Prep Associates and the founder of the *Don't Blow the Interview* workshop—an interview training program that is primarily targeted to college students, and is presented at colleges and universities. Inquiries regarding the workshop can be directed to interviewprep1@aol.com.

A lifelong New Yorker, he and his wife now reside in Savannah, Georgia.